D0805421

A
"BILL OF RIGHTS"
FOR CHILDREN

Publication Number 927

AMERICAN LECTURE SERIES

A Monograph in

AMERICAN LECTURES IN BEHAVIORAL SCIENCES AND LAW

Editor

RALPH SLOVENKO

Professor of Law
Wayne University Law School
Detroit, Michigan

A
"BILL OF RIGHTS"
FOR CHILDREN

By

HENRY H. FOSTER, JR.
School of Law
New York University
New York, New York

With a Foreword by

JUDGE JUSTINE WISE POLIER
Counsel for the Children's Defense Fund
New York City

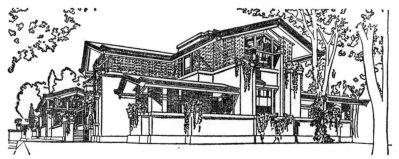

CHARLES C THOMAS • **PUBLISHER**
Springfield • *Illinois* • *U.S.A.*

Published and Distributed Throughout the World by
CHARLES C THOMAS • PUBLISHER
Bannerstone House
301-327 East Lawrence Avenue, Springfield, Illinois, U.S.A.

© *1974, by* CHARLES C THOMAS • PUBLISHER
ISBN 0-398-02985-7 (cloth)
0-398-02986-5 (paper)
Library of Congress Catalog Card Number: 73-12718

Printed in the United States of America
N-1

Library of Congress Cataloging in Publication Data

Foster, Henry Hubbard, 1911-
    A "Bill of rights" for children.

    (American lecture series, publication no. 927.
A monograph in American lectures in behavioral
sciences and law)
    1. Children-Law—United States. I. Title.
KF479.F68   346'.73'013   73-12718
ISBN 0-398-02985-7
ISBN 0-398-02986-5 (pbk.)

DEDICATION

Dedicated to my children, Ann Foster Pape and Robert A. Foster, who may well wish that I had practiced what I preach.

FOREWORD

A "Bill of Rights" for Children offers tonic and challenge to those concerned with both the welfare of children and their rights as children. It should provide tonic to opponents of ongoing efforts by the Federal Administration to curtail programs for the welfare of children through strategies for their attrition and the avoidance of national responsibility. It should provide a challenge to those battling against injustices practiced against children within various institutions, including the administration of justice, by the computerizing of children, or by the failure to see children as persons whose rights demand respect. Professor Foster's underlying thrust strikes at servile status of children which permits the adult world, through parents, teachers, voluntary agencies, or public arms of government to grant or withhold rights from children to which they should be entitled. So long as this is true, rights are reduced to uncertain privileges. It is only when rights are enforceable that they are truly rights.

Dissatisfied with vague and general talk about the rights of children, the author has undertaken the hard task of seeking to define what he sees as "specific rights" in four major areas affecting the lives of children. He supports "healthy skepticism" concerning the adjudicatory and correctional processes of juvenile courts. However, Professor Foster also realistically wrestles with how to achieve protections for children within what he sees as an adversary judicial system that will endure for a long time. In doing so he targets in on the denial of due process, the absence of independent counsel for children, and the failure to see children as persons, while those with power to determine their lives continue to utter pious platitudes, unsupported by sound practices.

In the light of the limited wisdom, skills and resources available, Professor Foster raises serious questions about the steady increase of state intervention in the lives of children and families. Like many others discouraged by the failures of schools, courts and institutions, the author seems to see diversion from the system as the only way to enhance the rights of children. Indeed, he goes so far as to conclude that "the combination of compulsory school attendance and child labor laws is a major factor contributing to unrest and crime in many city areas." Here, the burden of failure is placed on the laws rather than on the failure of government to provide quality education and real work opportunities. One must question whether discouragement with things as they are is not thus causing a lowering of sights as to what children are entitled to receive. Hopefully, such attacks on institutions that have failed will not be satisfied with restricting their roles, but will serve as a staging area for positive demands that such institutions shall fulfill their responsibilities to children.

As the author struggles to identify various and inconsistent legislative designations that determine children's rights, age level considerations by courts, and government interventions in the lives of children or their parents, he correctly describes a crazy quilt of action and nonaction in regard to children's rights. This crazy quilt reflects fundamental conflicts concerning the value we place on our children, despite the self-flattering myth that we are a child-centered society. It reflects the lack of consistent policies and practices, let alone a social philosophy, directed toward comprehensive programs to advance the welfare of children or protect their rights.

These lacks are evidenced by the fragmented, inconsistent and inadequate practices now pervasive: Parental abuse or neglect is subject to court action but not community abuse or neglect of dependent children. The right to counsel for delinquent children at an adjudicatory hearing has not yet been extended to provide a similar right to dependent or neglected children. The right to medical care does not include the right to minimal nutritional support. Workfare for poor mothers was sanctioned, while a comprehensive plan for day care was vetoed as threatening the sanctity of the family. Despite rhetoric about the importance of the family, the lowest level of assistance is given to the child in his own home, while more is provided when he is removed to live with strangers, and most is provided when he is institutionalized.

Ongoing discriminatory practices against children of minority groups continue on a spectrum, ranging from blatant to subtle, that affect every aspect of children's rights. They range from exclusion from protective or preventive services and from denial of foster care or adoption to token admission in what are regarded as the better services.

The battle to free children from archaic legal disabilities and establish rights for children in specific areas as presented in this volume provides a significant approach to the larger question of what needs to be done to provide all children in this country with the right and opportunity for healthy and full development.

A second important approach is reflected in the class actions, brought in recent years, to establish and protect the constitutional rights of children. These include actions against cruel and unusual punishment in custodial institutions, the denial of appropriate treatment in schools for the retarded, mental hospitals, and child caring institutions. They include actions against unlawful exclusions, suspensions and expulsions from school which deny a child's right to an education. They also include actions against discriminatory practices in violation of the Civil Rights Act and the constitutional guarantee of equal protection. These case by case battles are desperately needed and must be expanded to counter injustices wherever they are found. The need for them becomes more urgent as the Federal government minimizes its responsibility for enforcing compliance by the states so that their actions shall assure the constitutional rights of children.

There is, however, still a third area in which the rights of children must be asserted in new ways. It will require the development of policies and programs at every level of government directed to reaching out and providing aid and services to children of poverty for whom aid has been limited largely to the bare bones of inadequate public assistance. For the millions of children on the ADC rolls, no minimum national standards of assistance or "intervention" have been established. There are states which provide an average of only $14 to $20 monthly for the support of a child. It would seem that the developing concept of the "Right to Treatment" for persons deprived of freedom in the name of treatment must be enlarged to establish the right to appropriate aid and care for every child where there is state intervention, whether by administrative or judicial action.

Such a program may at first seem heresy to the non-interventionists who are now concentrating on how to divert children from a system that has woefully failed. Yet, to ignore the denial of minimum standards required for the wholesome development of children, would be all too reminiscent of the self-satisfaction of some agencies in regard to children in their care, and their failure to recognize that they were providing only miniscule islands of care in a large sea of neglect that was endangering children denied access to their services. I would rather believe that the author's concepts concerning *A "Bill of Rights" for Children* and the class action approach provide bases for developing far more comprehensive planning and programs for children. Such planning and programs will have to embrace not only emphasis on due process for children, an end of inappropriate legal disabilities, the challenge to injustices in individual cases, and the emergence of A Bill of Rights. It will also have to encompass the imposition of duties on parents, schools, administrative agencies, courts and the larger community to translate asserted rights into a program of substantive justice as the enforceable right of every child.

JUDGE JUSTINE WISE POLIER

PREFACE

THE ESTABLISHMENT, legal and otherwise, is grossly unfair to minors and they are becoming increasingly aware of that fact. The idea of fairness is part of the fabric of the doctrine of justice, and the sense of what's fair and unfair emerges in childhood. For our purposes, it makes little difference whether or not the child's conscience (or super ego) is developed primarily by identification with the father as psychoanalytic theory would have it, or through association with peers as asserted by Piaget and Sutherland, or both. In any event, children must be treated fairly if we want them to mature into responsible adulthood.

This means that we had best reckon with the child's point of view and his sense of fairness. The *Bill of Rights for Children* that follows is an attempt to specify some legitimate grievances currently existing and to develop new principles and guidelines for children and the law. The list of principles and the examples cited does not purport to be exhaustive; rather, it is open-ended, and may be supplemented by the experience and insights of others. The thesis running through this exposition is that children are *people* and deserve legal and adult recognition as such and that until such recognition is accorded, the generation gap will not be closed.

In championing the recognition of the moral and legal rights of children we may be faced at the outset with the opposition of those who decry *permissiveness* or blame John Dewey for the demise of the public school system. The "spare the rod, spoil the child" school of thought, often equated with common sense, has had more than enough time to demonstrate failures. We reject it out of hand. At the same time, however, we do not minimize the importance to child development of firm and fair discipline and affectionate guidance. We advocate moral and legal rights for children because in our legalistic society that may be the only way their humanity can be protected.

More discerning critics may object that we are attempting to shift the status of children in general to the adult end of the continuum and that children should have the right to childhood. The fallacy of this position is that imposition of a feudal or servile status on minors may be self-defeating and in practice inconsistent with our professed concern over their welfare. Children do have a right to childhood but it must be recognized that childhood is preliminary to adolescence and eventual adulthood and moreover it is the most crucial period in human development. It is also obvious that much depends upon one's definition of "childhood." The status of minority ordinarily endures until age twenty-one, or under recent legislation, until age eighteen. *The right to childhood* means something different when we look at the interests, claims, and desires of teen-agers as compared with puling babies or those in the latency period. But there are certain fundamentals that are constant, such as the interest in having independent counsel whenever the placement of a child is at stake, and the right to fair treatment from all those who are in authority.

The use of the title *A "Bill of Rights" for Children* is not new. Others in the past have used it and the United Nations has promulgated basic principles of human rights including those of children. However, this book grew out of a unique experience. In 1967 it was decided that the regular course in Family Law at New York University should be broken up into two separate but interrelated courses, the second being entitled Children and the Law. It was a pioneering effort. There was no compilation of materials available for Children and the Law, so we were forced to gather together material from divers sources. In surveying the decisions and statutes in the field, as well as relevant literature from social and behavioral science, it became clear that the feudal status of minority was oppressive and that the usual assumptions were open to question. There also was the analogy of the women's liberation movement and the fact of increasing rebellion by our youth. We found that they were not rebels without cause.

In short, this book reflects one person's reaction to obsolete legal concepts which have been perpetuated and imposed during a time of ferment and change. Some of the ideas or principles here expressed were first outlined by the author in a speech before the American Academy of Pediatrics in Chicago on October

18, 1971. Later, a preliminary attempt to distill and expound principles was contained in a three-part article by Foster and Freed, which appeared in The New York Law Journal on July 28, August 25, and September 29, 1972. Thereafter, this version was written and its substance was discussed at the Atlanta Conference of the Psychiatry and Law Committee of the American Psychiatric Association and the American Academy of Psychiatry and the Law on March 16, 1973.

This brief discussion of the moral and legal rights of children does not attempt to explore and cover the larger philosophical, educational, and counseling problems of youth apart from the legal process. Instead we have attempted to focus upon legal status and the administration of justice, which may be within our area of competence, with occasional references to relevant non-legal materials. Since we are writing from a lawyer's vantagepoint, it should not be surprising that we conclude that the most practical reform for immediate implementation is the provision of independent counsel for children in any case where their placement or welfare is at stake.

We make this recommendation not because of any all-out commitment to the adversary system but because we are convinced that the adversary system is here to stay, and given the system, independent representation is essential if one is to be heard.

Youth advocacy programs and the public service activities of younger members of the bar also will have their impact on the administration of juvenile justice. We already have reached the stage of healthy skepticism concerning the adjudication and correction processes of juvenile courts and institutions. The current emphasis is upon goals and consequences and the law and programs will be evaluated in terms of how they work. But in addition to our pragmatic concern, we should also review the premises and the philosophy that underpin law and custom in this field. Hopefully, this small book may provoke thought and discussion about the law's treatment of children so that the gap will be narrowed between our professed concern over their welfare and the actual treatment of children as it appears in the adult world.

HENRY H. FOSTER, JR.

A BILL OF RIGHTS

A CHILD HAS A *moral* right and should have a *legal* right:

1. To be regarded as *a person* within the family, at school, and before the law.
2. To receive parental love and affection, discipline and guidance, and to grow to maturity in a home environment which enables him to develop into a mature and responsible adult.
3. To be supported, maintained, and educated to the best of parental ability, in return for which he has the *moral* duty to honor his father and mother.
4. To receive fair treatment from all in authority and to be heard and listened to.
5. To earn and keep his own earnings, and to be *emancipated* from the parent-child relationship when that relationship has broken down and he has left home due to abuse, neglect, serious family conflict, or other sufficient cause, and when his best interests would be served by the termination of parental authority.
6. To be free of legal disabilities or incapacities save where such are convincingly shown to be necessary and protective of his actual best interests.
7. To seek and obtain medical care and treatment and counseling.
8. To receive special care, consideration, and protection in the administration of law and justice so that his best interests always are a paramount factor.

CONTENTS

A
"BILL OF RIGHTS"
FOR CHILDREN

CHAPTER ONE

INTRODUCTION

A PATERNALISTIC AMBIVALENCE is the marked characteristic of the law's treatment of children. From the child's point of view, inconsistent signals emanate from adult authority and he is put in a double bind. On the one hand, a child's welfare and best interests is professed to be a dominant social concern, but on the other, what the law giveth, the law taketh away.

There is an urgent need for a comprehensive re-examination of the legal status of minors. It may be, to borrow the word used by Holmes, that the traditional legal status of minority is "revolting."[1] As Gault[2] makes plain, children are not, as Blackstone would have it, "favorites of our courts of Justice,"[3] but rather all too often are the victims of adult authoritarianism.[4] Legal processes and doctrines which are applied to children do not always square with the egalitarian principles and constitutional protections accorded to adult criminals even though the former may have had a greater need for protection.[5]

Historical reasons and adult attitudes account for the law's

---

[1]Justice Holmes, in his "The Path of the Law," *Harv L Rev, 10:*457, 1896, said "It is revolting to have no better reason for a rule of law than that so it was laid down in the time of Henry IV. It is still more revolting if the grounds upon which it was laid down have vanished long since, and the rule simply persists from blind imitation of the past."

[2]In the Matter of Gault, 387 U.S. 1 (1967).

[3]Erlich's Blackstone 89 (1959).

[4]The most critical recent evaluation of the juvenile court process is that by Forer, *No One Will Lissen* (1971).

[5]See Midonick: *Children, Parents and the Courts* (1972), for a detailed comparison of juvenile and criminal procedures and the applicability of due process of law concepts in juvenile court.

3

different treatment of children.[6] Some relics of feudalism have been perpetuated, as in the case of sex discrimination,[7] in terms of protectiveness.[8] We inherited a common law concept of status derived from a feudal order which denied children legal identity and treated them as objects or things, rather than as persons. Chancery, with its vague doctrine of *parens patriae*,[9] and occasional interventions by ecclesiastical courts,[10] accorded only a slight amelioration of a paternalistic common law.

The nineteenth century effected an uncertain compromise in

---

[6]Until the last century, children were regarded as an economic asset and the father had the prerogatives of ownership in his children. According to Blackstone, a male at twelve years old may take the oath of allegiance; at fourteen he is at years of discretion; at seventeen he may be an executor; and at twenty-one is at his own disposal and may alien his lands, goods, and chattels. A female at seven may be betrothed or given in marriage; at nine she is entitled to dower, at twelve she is at years of maturity, and therefore may consent or disagree to marriage, and, if proved to have sufficient discretion, may bequeath her personal estate; at seventeen she may be executrix; and at twenty-one she may dispose of herself and her lands. "So that full age in male and female is twenty-one years, which age is completed on the day preceding the anniversary of a person's birth; who till that time is an infant, and so styled in law." Ehrlich's Blackstone 98 (1959).

[7]See Kanowitz: *Women and the Law* (1968), especially Chapter three where he discusses coverture.

[8]Blackstone contends ". . . [but] their very disabilities are privileges; in order to secure them from hurting themselves by their own inprovident acts." Ehrlich's Blackstone 98 (1959 ed.). See Prince v. Massachusetts, 321 U.S. 158 (1944), where parental control is held to be subordinate to child labor regulations that are assumed to protect children. For a discussion of the labor movement's backing of child labor laws and compulsory education, in part to eliminate low wage competition, see Hartz: *Economic Policy and Democratic Thought*, p. 187 ff. (1948).

[9]The phrase parens patriae is taken from chancery practice where it was used to describe the power of the Crown to act *in loco parentis* in order to protect the person or property interests of infants. See Paulsen, Kent. v. United States: The Constitutional Context of Juvenile Cases, 1966 Sup. Ct. Review 167, 173. Pollock and Maitland: *History of English Law*, vol II, pp. 436-37 (2 ed. 1959), observe that "In the seventh century even the church was compelled to allow that in a case of necessity an English father might sell into slavery a son who was not yet seven years old. An older boy could not be sold without his consent. When he was thirteen or fourteen he might sell himself. From this we may gather that over his young children a father's power had been large; perhaps it extended to the killing of a child who had not yet tasted food. . . . Young girls might be given in marriage (or even in a case of necessity sold as slaves) against their will. It [the common law] looked at guardianship and paternal power merely as profitable rights, and had only sanctioned them when they could be made profitable." *Id.* at 444.

[10]See Greenspan v. Slate, 12 N.J. 426, 97 A.2d 390 (1953).

public policies applicable to children. Although the legal status of minors remained unchanged, the state interposed itself so as to limit and restrict the authority of the paterfamilias.[11] Compulsory education and child labor laws were enacted in several states[12] and at the *fin de siecle* the first juvenile courts were created.[13] Such measures were intended to serve the welfare of minors and to protect them from exploitation. However, the state's assertion of *parens patriae* powers constituted another kind of paternalism and an imposition of additional authority upon relatively helpless subordinates. The school teacher and the juvenile court judge became additional authority figures for regimented adolescents.

The last century also saw the demise of the common law notion that the father always should have custody of his children[14] (if he wanted it) and the emergence of the vague *best interests of the child* standard.[15] In application, however, the standard resulted in an automatic preference for the mother, assuming she was morally fit, with no meaningful inquiry being made into the child's best interests.[16] The mother simply had gained the proprietary interest in children that once had been the father's, and adult social or economic interests controlled the disposition of custody

---

[11]See Katz: *When Parents Fail* pp. 5-6 (1971).

[12]Hartz note 8.

[13]The first juvenile court was established in Cook County, Illinois, in 1899, as the result of the recommendations of the legal and social work professions. See Mack: *The juvenile court, Harv L Rev, 23*:104, 1909.

[14]According to Blackstone, the father (and in some cases the mother) is guardian by nature of the child and also a guardian for nurture until the child reached the age of fourteen years. The lord chancellor is, by right derived from the crown, the general and supreme guardian of all infants. See Ehrlich's *Blackstone* pp. 96-97 (1959). See also King v. DeManneville, 5 East 221, 102 Eng. Rep. 1054 (K.B. 1804); and Rex v. Greenhill, 4 A. & E. 624 (1836). In Shelley v. Westbrooke, 37 Eng. Rep. 850 (Ch. 1817), the court broke with precedent and refused to turn over children to the father, Percy Shelley, because of his alleged immoral conduct and way of life and unpopular political and religious views.

[15]The most influential American cases were the opinion by later Mr. Justice Brewer in Chapsky v. Wood, 26 Kan. 650, 40 Am. Rep. 321 (1881), and Justice Cardozo in Finlay v. Finlay, 240 N.Y. 429, 148 N.E. 624 (1925).

[16]See Drinan: *The rights of children in modern American family law, J Fam L, 2*:101, 1962; and Clark: *Law of Domestic Relations* (1968), p. 585.

cases. The custodial preference of the child was only a minor factor to be considered.[17]

The same arguments that were advanced for and against the abolition of slavery and the emancipation of women recur when issues arise regarding the moral and legal rights of children.[18] In the larger sense, there is a conflict between the principles of subordination and equality which are characteristic of a society that traces its origins to a patriarchal culture.[19] The recent lowering of voting age[20] and in some states the reduction of the age of majority[21] show that the movement from subordination to equality is gradual. Of course, complete autonomy for children to date has not been the accepted or desirable social goal. Perhaps youth must serve an apprenticeship. At the same time, however, children must be given some responsibility and freedom if we want them to develop into free and responsible adults. Most important, the adult establishment needs to review existing laws and statutes in order to determine whether they really protect and promote the welfare of children or primarily serve some adult interest or prejudice.

It also is necessary at the outset to make it clear that when reference is made to the *rights of children* we are making a general classification in terms of minority and in so doing follow

---

[17]See People v. Glendening, 259 App. Div. 384, 19 N.Y.S.2d 693 (1940), but compare Smith v. Smith, 15 Utah 2d 36, 386 P.2d 900 (1963), construing the Utah statute (Utah Code Ann. (1953) f 30-3-5).

[18]Compare the opinion by Mr. Justice Bradley in Bradwell v. State, 16 Wall. 130 (1872), which held that women could be denied the right to practice law, and Muller v. Oregon, 208 U.S. 412 (1908), where the *Brandeis brief* convinced the Court that a ten hour day for female factory workers was justifiable as a protection measure. In United States v. F.W. Darby Lumber Co., 312 U.S. 100 (1941), the child labor provisions of the Wage and Hour Act were sustained more as a restriction on unfair competition than as protection for the health and welfare of children.

[19]See Bryce: *Marriage and Divorce Under Roman and English Law, II Studies in History and Jurisprudence* p. 470 (1901). Reprinted in *III Select Essays in Anglo-American History* (1909).

[20]The Twenty-Sixth Amendment lowered the voting age to eighteen. See also Oregon v. Mitchell, 400 U.S. 112 (1970), sustaining the Voting Rights Act of 1970, which fixed the voting age at eighteen for voting in federal elections.

[21]As of 1972, approximately twenty states had lowered the age of majority from twenty-one to age eighteen.

the tradition of the law. This does not mean, however, that all members of the general class should receive identical treatment as to all matters concerning minority.[22] An age differential may justify legal distinctions based upon chronological age if the stage of maturation has relevance to the particular problem. Thus, presumably it is not unconstitutional or discriminatory to set a reasonable age regarding consent for marriage,[23] for driving an automobile,[24] or for hazardous employment.[25] Unless the age specified is completely out of kilter with prevailing mores, some leeway must be accorded for legislative judgment. The discussion that follows, for the most part, will be concerned with claimed moral and legal rights for children, *i.e.* those having the status of minority, although for some matters such as child custody or due process in juvenile court, obviously a particular sub-group may be most involved with the particular problem. We will now consider the specific rights we have postulated.

---

[22]"The Constitution does not require things which are different in fact or opinion to be treated in law as though they were the same." Mr. Justice Frankfurter in Tigner v. Texas, 310 U.S. 141, 147 (1940).

[23]See Foster: Marriage: a "basic civil right of man," *Fordham L Rev*, 37:51, 72, 1968. However, an equal protection argument may be made where a statute without justification sets different ages for marriage based upon sex. For example, see Vlasak v. Vlasak, 204 Minn. 331, 283 N.W. 489 (1939).

[24]For example, see Perry v. Simione, 107 Cal 132, 239 P. 1056 (1925).

[25]Under the Fair Labor Standards Act (29 U.S.C. 203 (1)) employment of a minor in hazardous employments may be "oppressive child labor."

CHAPTER TWO

TO BE REGARDED AS A *PERSON*

THE TRADITIONAL ATTITUDE AND NORMS of the law regarding minors is reflected in the fact that they are not regarded as legal persons even though our materialistic society has given such status to corporations.[26] Minors thus are classified by the law along with the seriously mentally ill and criminals who have been deprived of civil rights.[27] No matter how benevolent the intent, the deprivation has serious consequences, for the child's moral right to be regarded as a person is basic to the other rights which follow. If minors secure status as legal persons, and if this fundamental principle were accepted, appreciated, and implemented, our other rights of children would fall neatly into place.

A great deal of the difficulty in our treatment of minors, legal and otherwise, stems from our refusal to accept them as individuals, with their own needs, interests, and desires. It does not take a good memory to recall the communication and attitudinal problems youth encounter when dealing with adults.[28] Despite any and all evidence to the contrary, the inferiority of youth is assumed by those who speak with *the voice of experience*. An authoritarian adult not only swings his weight around, he makes explicit the inferior status of minority.

---

[26]Despite the argument by Mr. Justice Black in Connecticut General Life Insurance Co. v. Johnson, 303 U.S. 77 (1938), that the word *person* in the Fourteenth Amendment does not include corporations.

[27]One of the most anomalous vestiges of ancient law is the doctrine of civil death when a party receives a life sentence, as in New York, and the other partner to the marriage has an option to regard the marriage as terminated, without need for a judicial decree. See In re Lindwall's Will, 287 N.Y. 347, 39 N.E.2d 907, 139 A.L.R. 1301 (1942), and Note: Civil deaths—medieval fiction in a modern world, *Harv. L. Rev. 50*:968, 1937. See also Condit and Liebenow: Management of estates of minors and incompetents, *U. Ill. L. F.* 268, 1951; Fraser: Guardianship of the person, *Iowa L. Rev., 45*:239, 1960; and Fratcher: Powers and duties of guardians of property, *Iowa L. Rev. 45*:264, 1960.

[28]See Forer: *No One Will Lissen* (1971).

It is curious that parents, judges, police, and t͟
relations with children, often behave in authoritari͟
matter how respectful they may be in coping with ͟
Acton's famous maxim that power tends to corrupt a͟
power corrupts absolutely may have some relevanc͟
phenomenon.[29] Children are often scapegoats for adult
tions.[30] But the worst of all is hypocrisy—a vice readily disc͟nible
by youth. They are specialists at detecting it in adults no matter
how charitable they may be with regard to the hypocrisy of their
peers. We use the term *Hypocrisy* because invariably adults dispense denials and punishments in terms of *it's for your own good,*
no matter what the circumstances, and when the situation really
is one where *might makes right.*[31]

Authority carries with it added responsibility and where adults
deal with children there is a moral obligation of fairness and
empathy. The relative helplessness and lack of autonomy of young
children requires both self-restraint and legal checks on parental
and other authority. Moreover, if children are persons, their
points of view merit consideration; adult decisions should be
reasoned and ordinarily explained; and the actual best interests
of children should be reckoned with in terms of reality rather
than fantasy.[32]

The ideal for adult behavior here expressed does not imply
that minors are incapable of wrong doing or should be immune
from accountability for their actions. On the contrary, the more
self-determination and responsibility that is accorded to minors,
the greater the accountability. To stipulate a *bill of rights* for
children does not free them from moral and legal obligations but
is intended to enhance their sense of responsibility. If they are

[29]Letter to Bishop Mandell Creighton, April 5, 1887.

[30]Goldstein and Katz: *The Family and the Law* (1965,) use the transcript, motions,
and decisions in the case of Lesser v. Lesser as a basis for demonstrating the psychological dimension of a bitter contest over divorce and custody, where children
are used as pawns in a continuing conflict.

[31]For an extreme example, see Stehr v. State, 92 Neb. 755, 139 N.W. 676 (1913),
which affirmed a manslaughter conviction where a stepfather permitted his stepson
to freeze because the latter had wet the bed.

[32]See Foster: Adoption and child custody: best interests of the child?, *Buffalo L.
Rev. 22:*1, 9, 1972.

fairly treated as human beings they are entitled to a reckoning even though compassion may mitigate their due, and regard for pragmatic consequences may suspend the application of a heavy hand.[33]

Authoritarian behavior by adults is not limited to the home. Some but not all teachers and school administrators are martinets and a few judges have been known to have a *Jehovah's complex*.[34] There also are some arbitrary case workers and bureaucrats who complicate the lives of children.[35] The authoritarian adult, whatever his or her profession, treats minors as inferiors, withholds respect, and regards them as objects of sufferance. Thus the adult's own frustrations may be relieved by the prerogative of seniority he assumes in dealing with children.

The Judeo-Christian belief in the dignity of man does not have a cut-off point based on age. Neither does a belief in the sacredness of man and the integrity of the individual. To fail to treat a minor as a person, at home, in school, or before the law, is to deny his humanity.

Achievement of status as legal persons means that minors would receive independent consideration of their individual interests by the law and those in authority. They could sue and be sued in their own name and could intervene in proceedings involving their own welfare.[36] Rather than a guardian or next friend controlling the matter, the minor and his counsel would make relevant decisions. Instead of the current emphasis on relational interests of parents in their children,[37] if minors became *sui juris*, and were real parties in interest, there would be greater autonomy for them and an assurance that their point of view would be presented. The implications of this will become more apparent when we discuss emancipation and related problems.

---

[33]Studies of violent children confirm that usually they were brutalized by parents. For example, see Freeman and Hulse: *Children Who Kill* (1962).

[34]Although this syndrome is unknown to the nomenclature of psychiatry it is a phenomenon known to practicing lawyers.

[35]For example, see In re Rinker: 117 A.2d 780 (Pa. Super 1955).

[36]See Speca and Wehrman: Protecting the rights of children in divorce cases in Missouri, *U M K C L Rev*, 38:1, 1969.

[37]See Note: Alternatives to parental right in custody disputes involving third persons, *Yale L J*, 73:151, 1963.

CHAPTER THREE

TO RECEIVE PARENTAL LOVE AND AFFECTION

Discipline and guidance, and to grow to maturity
in a home environment which enables him to develop into a mature and responsible adult.

THE NEED OF A CHILD FOR parental love and affection is so
thoroughly documented by clinical and common experience
and the literature of behavioral science that it may be accepted
as an established fact.[38] It is also agreed, but not so evident, that
children need discipline and guidance.[39] Difficulty arises when we
try to apply such generalizations. Whose standards are applicable?

Until quite recently, the law presumed that children received
love and affection in the home and that instances of child abuse
or emotional deprivation were exceedingly rare. It is now known
that such a presumption is a dangerous one to make and that
parental brutality, rejection, or indifference is quite common.

[38]For example, see Watson: The children of Armageddon: problems of custody
following divorce, *Syracuse L Rev, 21:55,* 1969; and Note: Alternatives to parental
right in child custody disputes involving third parties, *Yale L J, 73:*151, 1963. See
also, the United Nations Declaration of Rights of Children, adopted unanimously
on November 20, 1959. Principle six provides: "The child, for the full and har-
monious development of his personality, needs love and understanding. He shall,
whenever possible, grow up in the care and under the responsibility of his parents,
and, in any case, in an atmosphere of affection and of moral and material security."

[39]"To assist in the development of respect for authority, courts give parents
wide latitude in the exercise of disciplinary powers. An underlying reason for this
latitude is the belief that one way in which children learn to adjust to the man-
dates of society is through the proper use of discipline." Katz: *When Parents
Fail* (1971) p. 13. See also Mahler: Discipline and punishment. Reprinted in Goldstein and Katz: *The Family and the Law* (1965), pp. 977-980, who says: " . . . [a]
certain measure of discipline is indispensable for the child's sake as an individual,
as a member of the family and as a future member of society. The primary and
essential goal of modern education is to strengthen the child's self or ego."

The *battered child syndrome* has received extensive publicity and parental rejection is a frequent theme of both professional literature and fiction.[40] The speed with which legislatures enacted child abuse legislation requiring the reporting of suspected cases is virtually without precedent.[41] Every American jurisdiction recently has enacted a statute covering the *battered child syndrome* although such statutes vary in their terms.[42] This legislation supplements prior laws dealing with dependent and neglected children and a typical state will have several different statutes on the general subject of child abuse and neglect and alternative criminal and civil sanctions which may be used against a culpable parent.[43]

The law, however, has shied away from extending statutes which cover physical abuse to instances of psychological abuse or emotional deprivation.[44] This is somewhat curious. With regard to the husband-wife relation, the law has evolved a concept of cruelty which may embrace the most subtle kinds of psychological warfare.[45] Usually such has been done at the behest of a plaintiff-wife in a divorce case[46] although a husband may establish cruelty in some states by proving that the wife engaged in a so-called *speaking strike* (the *silent treatment*),[47] falsely accused him of infidelity,[48] unreasonably refused to have sexual relations,[49] or

---

[40]One of the most highly publicized cases involving parental rejection was the custody dispute over Gloria Vanderbilt who was placed with her aunt rather than her mother. See Matter of Vanderbilt, 245 App. Div. 211, 281 N.Y.S. 171 (1935). See also, Foster and Freed: The battered child, *Trial, 3:*33, 1967.

[41]See Paulsen: The legal framework for child protection, *Col L Rev, 66:*679, 681-84, 1966.

[42]See Paulsen, Parker and Adelman: Child abuse reporting laws — some legislative history, *Geo Wash L Rev, 34:*482, 1966, and McCord: Battered child. *Minn L Rev, 50:*1, 1965.

[43]*Ibid.*

[44]For exceptional cases, see Jones v. Koulos, 142 Colo. 92, 349 P.2d 704 (1960), and Application of Mittenthal, 37 Misc. 2d 502, 235 N.Y.S.2d 729 (Fam. Ct. 1962).

[45]See Clark: *Law of Domestic Relations* (1968) pp. 346-48.

[46]See Foster and Freed: *Law and the Family—New York,* 1972 rev. ed., §6:11.

[47]Although Reinhard v. Reinhard, 96 Wis. 555, 71 N.W. 803 (1897), and Hiecke v. Hiecke, 163 Wis. 171, 157 N.W. 747 (1916), involved speaking strikes by the husband the court said such silence by a spouse was cruelty.

[48]See Clark: *Law of Domestic Relations* (1968), p. 347.

[49]*Ibid.*

subjected him to verbal abuse.[50] For a variety of reasons, there has been no similar extension of child abuse or neglect.

There have been, however, a few custody cases where psychological detriment or advantage has been crucial. As courts become increasingly sophisticated as to psychiatric principles, the number of such cases will increase substantially. An example is a New York case where a *smothering mother* upon her release from a mental hospital sought to regain custody of her seventeen year old son.[51] The boy, while living with his overly-protective and interfering mother (a virtual Mrs. Portnoy) had done poorly in school and in social adjustments. While in foster home care and free from her dominance, his school work improved and he became better adjusted. The court followed the stated preference of the son and dismissed the mother's habeas corpus action, but with leave for her to reapply at a later time after the son had completed his high school studies. The court conceded that the petitioner was a "fit" mother apart from being "impatient and aggressive" with her only child but found that the son's interests would be best served by continuing the foster home and school arrangement. It is to be noted, however, that this case did not involve an allegation of neglect and it was not a final determination of the mother's custodial rights.

Where a neglect petition is brought, despite the broad language of such statutes,[52] courts generally are loath to make a finding of neglect on the basis of emotional deprivation or psychological detriment because of the permanent character of such decisions as compared with custody orders which always are sub-

---

[50]*Ibid.*, at 348.

[51]Application of Mittenthal, 37 Misc.2d 502, 235 N.Y.S.2d 729 (Fam. Ct. 1962).

[52]See for example, N.Y. Family Court Act § 312 which provides that "A neglected child means a male less than sixteen years of age or a female less than eighteen years of age (a) whose parent . . . does not adequately supply the child with food, clothing, shelter, education, or medical or surgical care, though financially able or offered financial means to do so; or (b) who suffers or is likely to suffer serious harm from improper guardianship, including lack of moral supervision or guidance. . .; or (c) who has been abandoned or deserted by his parents. . . ." A comparable age differential between males and females was sustained in Lamb v. State, 475 P.2d 829 (Okla. Crim. App. 1970).

ject to modification due to changed circumstances.[53] It is fair to say that in neglect cases egregious parental unfitness rather than the best interests of the child is the ultimate issue. Usually there must be abandonment, serious physical abuse or gross immorality that directly affects the child, and emotional deprivation or parental rejection will not be enough.[54] Moreover, in neglect cases, there is the problem of reasonable alternatives and the lack of assurance that placement out of the home would be any improvement for an unhappy child. Unless physical injury or death is threatened, it may be deemed practical to leave the child where he is and to attempt to induce the family to participate in counseling.

In the case of the parent's right to give and the child's right to receive discipline and guidance, we again have the problems of standards. One danger is that courts, or case workers, will inflexibly apply middle-class mores without regard to the circumstances of the particular family.[55] Obviously, methods of discipline differ, and parents tend to repeat those forms of punishment that they were subjected to by their own parents.[56] Beyond that, however, the more recent cases have diminished the parental privilege of corporal punishment and have passed upon its necessity as well as its alleged excessiveness in the individual case.[57] The same is true of correction by those who stand *in loco parentis,* such as school authorities.[58]

Although the adage "spare the rod, spoil the child" is in general disrepute, there is agreement that a firm and consistent discipline

---

[53]See Comment: Termination of Parental Rights to Free child for Adoption, N.Y.U. L. Rev. *32:*579, 584, 1957.

[54]*Ibid.*

[55]See in re Rinker, 117 A.2d 780 (Pa. Super. 1955).

[56]"There are men whose cruelty seems to permeate all of their life relationships, rather than just their relationships with women. In my experience men of this type, without exception, have been treated cruelly in early life. They generally have had a brutal father, with whom they formed a lasting and blighting identification, but in some instances this may be the mother." Guttmacher: *The Mind of the Murderer.* (1960), p. 96.

[57]See State v. Straight, 347 P.2d 482 (Mont. 1959).

[58]See Nelson: Right of a teacher to administer corporal punishment to a student, *Wash. L. J., 5:*75, 1965.

is essential for proper ego control, maturation, and socialization.[59] The lack of proper disciplining, however, ordinarily is not subject to judicial review unless accompanied by juvenile *acting out* outside the home, in which event, the child may be processed as a person in need of supervision (PINS) or as an incorrigible.[60]

Parental failure to give moral guidance or the setting of a bad example may constitute one form of neglect[61] or gross parental immorality may clinch the result of a contest over custody.[62] The more recent decisions, however, insist that such immorality must have some direct bearing on the child's welfare.[63] The discreet affair, outside the home, may be a divorced or separated parent's own business.

A recent unreported New York case may illustrate the problem. The separated father and mother had three children: a daughter in her late teens who was away at school, a daughter of twelve, and a son aged nine. The mother, by agreement, had custody of the three children, and the father paid her an agreed upon sum for wife and child support, and also had visitation rights weekends and holidays. He rented a brownstone in Greenwich Village where he lived with the young lady he intended to marry when he secured a divorce based upon separation. The three children stayed with them on weekends and holidays. With good reason the children were afraid of their mother who for some time had been under psychiatric care. She had frequent rows with the two younger children and would try to beat them, throw objects at them, and would fly into rages. One such scene was repeated in the presence of the psychiatrist who was attempting family counseling. Upon a later occasion, following a particularly violent episode, the two younger children telephoned their father

---

[59]Cf. note 39.

[60]See Glueck: *The Problem of Delinquency* (1959), pp. 322-33. Perhaps the most extreme statute is the Massachusetts so-called *stubborn child* statute. See Commonwealth v. Brasher, 270 N.E.2d 389 (Mass. 1971), sustaining Mass. Gen. Law c. 277 §53 as amended by St. 1959, c. 304, §1. See also Sidman: The Massachusetts Stubborn Child Law: Law and Order in the Home, *Fam. L.Q., 6:33*, 1972.

[61]Cf. note 52.

[62]*Ibid.*

[63]See Ploscowe, Foster, and Freed: *Family Law*, 1972 rev. ed., pp. 913-15.

to come and pick them up. He did so and then started a habeas corpus action to obtain full custodial rights to all three children.

The case was tried before a judge who was a spinster of retirement age. During the course of the trial it became obvious that the judge, while disapproving of the living arrangements of the father, was more astonished by the forthrightness of their testimony, their evident good character, and the fine relationship they had with the children as compared with the chaotic conditions in the mother's home. The psychiatric testimony and a questioning of the children led to a custody award to the father even before he had secured his divorce and had remarried. Visitation rights were accorded to the mother. This decision is quite unusual, everything considered, and it illustrates an emphasis of psychological factors in determining the best interests of the children.[64]

The child's right to parental love and affection is meaningful only if those terms are defined psychologically. By *parental love* is meant the affectionate relationship between those who stand in the position of parent and child. This does not necessarily mean the biological parents and child, but may mean those who have such a psychological relationship.[65] It is the on-going nurturing care and attention, not biological birth, which gives rise to real mother love.[66]

The development of such a bond of attachment between *de facto* parents and child should always be a crucial factor in resolving difficult custody and adoption cases. Unfortunately, such is not always the case. *Raymond v. Cotner*[67] is a deplorable example of last century thinking in custody cases. In that case the father and mother were divorced when Lin Dee was fifteen months old and previously had separated shortly after her birth. Mother and

---

[64]See Note: Alternatives to parental right in custody disputes involving third parties, *Yale L J*, 73:151, 157-169, 1963, for a discussion of the phychological well-being of a child as the determinent in deciding the best interests of the child.

[65]See In re Adoption of a Child by P and Wife, 114 N.J. Super 584, 277 A.2d 566 (1971), and In re Revocation of Appointment of a Guardian of a Minor Surrendered for Adoption, — Mass.—, 271 N.E. 2d 621 (1971).

[66]See Foster, Adoption and child custody: Best interests of the child? *Buffalo L Rev*, 22:1, at 13, 1972.

[67]175 Neb. 158, 120 N.W.2d 892 (1963).

daughter moved in with the maternal grandparents and the mother obtained a full time job. The grandparents raised the child and when Lin Dee was eleven her mother was killed in an automobile accident. Within a few months the natural father brought a habeas corpus action to obtain the custody of Lin Dee. The father had visited Lin Dee when she was small but had not seen her for the past nine years, although he lived less than one hundred miles away. He paid all the child support required by the divorce decree but had not communicated with his daughter. At the trial she tearfully testified that she wanted to stay with the grandparents and her friends and did not want to move in with her father and his second wife and family.

The majority of the Nebraska Supreme Court held that the father had a superior right to custody unless it had been forfeited by abandonment, complete indifference, or by his becoming an unfit parent.[68] Only if his natural (property?) right had been forfeited, should his claim give way to the best interests of the child. The dissent pointed out that in effect the majority had held that a fit parent has the *exclusive* right to custody of his child.[69]

Although there are many older cases and a few recent ones[70] that support the majority opinion in *Raymond v. Cotner* it is interesting to note that subsequent Nebraska cases reject that decision without overruling it by name[71] and that where courts are directed towards the psychological aspects of the relationships, by testimony and argument, the de facto parents usually prevail.[72] A lamentable exception occurred at the original hearing in the so-called *Baby Lenore* case in New York.[73]

In the *Baby Lenore* Case, the natural mother was a native of Columbia, 32 years old, a college graduate, who was employed in

[68]*Ibid.*, p. 895.

[69]Dissenting opinion *Ibid.*, at 896.

[70]See cases collected in Annot., 25 A.L.R.3d 1 (1969), involving contests between a natural parent and grandparents.

[71]See In re Application of Carlson, 181 Neb. 877, 152 N.W.2d 98, 25 A.L.R.3d 1 (1967).

[72]Cf. note 65.

[73]People ex rel. Scarpetta v. Spence-Chapin Adoption Service, 36 App. Div.2d 524, 317 N.Y.S.2d 928, aff'd 28 N.Y.2d 185, 269 N.E.2d 787, 321 N.Y.S.2d 65 (1971).

a responsible professional position.[74] She also had $20,000 in the bank. In January she consulted an adoption agency in New York, telling the counselor that she wished to place her baby for adoption immediately after birth. She had some fourteen counseling sessions with the agency before the child's birth in May. Six different alternatives were suggested for consideration, including placing the child in temporary care while she took more time to make up her mind. The mother steadfastly insisted that she wanted to place the child for adoption and thirteen days after Baby Lenore was born the mother executed a formal surrender, in the presence of her sister, which document gave the agency authority to place the child in an adoptive home and to consent to her adoption. The mother had not seen the baby since birth.

Some twenty-five days later, a friend of the mother telephoned the agency to report that the mother was uncertain about whether she had done the right thing and "felt unfulfilled." Within a few days the mother had another interview with the agency and according to the counselor's testimony did not demand return of the baby but merely complained about her mixed feelings regarding the surrender. In the interim, one month after birth, and eighteen days after execution of the surrender, Baby Lenore was delivered to the adoptive parents. This was a week before the agency was called regarding the natural mother's possible change of mind. The mother consulted a psychiatrist for three months, then a lawyer, and a habeas corpus action was brought to regain the child. The adoptive parents knew nothing about these developments until two months later, when Baby Lenore had been in their home for five months.[75]

The New York proceedings involved a contest between the natural mother and the adoption agency. The adoptive parents sought leave to intervene and were denied that right. The case itself was tried as a contract matter, the testimony and arguments

---

[74]The facts stated in the text are taken from the transcript in the New York case or were testified to in the Florida proceeding. The author participated in the Florida proceeding on behalf of the adoptive family. The Florida cases are reported in Scarpetta v. DiMartino, 254 So.2d 813 (Fla. Dist. Ct. App. 1971), 262 So.2d 442 (Fla. Sup. Ct. 1972), cert. denied 93 S. Ct. 437 (1973).

[75]*Ibid.*

being directed at the issue of whether or not the mother had a privilege to revoke her consent to placement of the child for adoption at any time before a final adoption decree.[76] There was not a scintilla of evidence regarding the best interests of Baby Lenore. It was held that the mother was privileged to revoke her consent to placement for adoption and the case eventually reached the highest court of New York.[77]

There are many troublesome things about the New York decision. The Court of Appeals stated its approval of the doctrine that the best interests of the child controlled and that there was no absolute right to revoke a consent to adoption where no fraud or undue influence had been shown.[78] However, since there was no evidence in the record bearing directly on the best interests of Baby Lenore, the court resorted to the presumption that a child's best interests would be served by placement with its mother.[79] Moreover, it affirmed the denial of leave to intervene by the adoptive parents even though they were most qualified to give evidence regarding the best interests of Baby Lenore. The actual issue became the fitness of the natural mother, and finding her to be a fit person, it followed that the baby must be returned to her.[80]

The sequel, of course, was that the would-be adoptive parents having been rebuffed by the law resorted to self-help and fled with the child to Florida. In Florida, a second trial occurred, this time between the mother and the adoptive parents. Counsel for the mother argued that the child should be returned to the mother because of the New York decision and because a contempt citation had been issued when the adoptive parents fled from New York. Thus they were "outlaws." Attorneys for the adoptive parents sought to establish that the child's welfare required that she remain with the adoptive parents. Prominent psy-

---

[76]*Ibid.*

[77]People ex rel. Scarpetta v. Spence-Chapin Adoption Service, 28 N.Y.2d 185, 269 N.E. 2d 787, 321 N.Y.S.2d 65 (1971), cert. den. 404 U.S. 805 (1971).

[78]269 N.E.2d at 790.

[79]269 N.E.2d at 792.

[80]*Ibid.*

chiatrists,[81] pediatricians, and psychologists testified concerning the detriment which might be occasioned by removal from surrogate parents when a child is between twelve and eighteen months old,[82] and those who had interviewed the family testified concerning the good relationship between Baby Lenore and the adoptive family.[83] The trial court dismissed the writ, holding that the child's welfare controlled and that it would best be served by Baby Lenore remaining in the only home she had ever known.[84] Subsequent appeals were unsuccessful[85] and presumably in due time a Florida adoption decree will be entered so as to settle all issues. If, however, the adoptive parents return to New York they may face contempt citations.[86]

The legal and social implications of the Baby Lenore case are far reaching. The New York legislature's response was to change the statutory law of adoption so as to overrule both the reasoning and the holding of the Court of Appeals.[87] The new legislation reemphasizes the legal and practical distinction between private and agency placements and differentiates the two processes. Adoption agencies were threatened by the court's language in the Baby Lenore case (that there was no distinction between private

---

[81]Witnesses appearing for the DiMartino family included Drs Stella Chess, Jay Katz, and Andrew Watson, among others. The gist of their testimony was that especially at Baby Lenore's age (then a little over a year) it might be traumatic to remove her from a warm and loving home and return her to the natural mother who contemplated engaging a "nanny" in her late sixties (who could not speak English) to take care of the child while the mother was employed. For a further discussion of the danger of removing a child in such a situation, see Foster: Adoption and Child Custody: Best Interests of the Child?, *Buffalo L. Rev.*, 22:1, 12-13, 1972.

[82]See Bowlby: *Attachment and Loss* (1969), p. 223; Chess: *An Introduction to Child Psychiatry* (1969), p. 16; Patton: *Growth Failure in Maternal Deprivation* (1963), p. 38.

[83]Dr. Stella Chess interviewed the family and Baby Lenore for several hours before testifying in the Florida case. The child's pediatrician also testified.

[84]254 So.2d 813 (1972).

[85]262 So.2d 442, cert. denied 93 S. Ct. 437 (1973).

[86]It is interesting to note that although Mr. DiMartino may be in contempt of the New York order to return Baby Lenore to the natrual mother, nonetheless he was admitted to the Florida Bar.

[87]Laws 1972, Ch. 639, amended New York Dom. Rel. Law §§ 115-116 (McKinney Supp. 1972), and N.Y. Soc. Serv. Law §§ 383-384 (McKinney Supp. 1972).

placements and agency placements[88]) and were shocked by the court's use of the presumption that a child's welfare would best be served by placement with the natural mother under the facts of the case. Such was regarded as a threat to the integrity of the adoption process in New York.

The new statute provides that natural parents "shall have no right to the custody of such child superior to that of adoptive parents" even if they are "fit, competent and able to duly maintain, support and educate the child. The custody of such a child [surrendered for adoption or placed in an adoptive home] shall be awarded solely on the basis of the best interests of the child, and there shall be no presumption [as in the Baby Lenore case] that such interests will be promoted by any particular custodial disposition."[89] Except where there are allegations of fraud, duress or coercion in the execution or inducement of a surrender for adoption, there are strict limitations on the commencement of an action to revoke consent to adoption or to regain a child who was surrendered for that purpose. If the surrender so states, no such actions may be brought if the child has been placed in an adoptive home and more than thirty days have elapsed since the surrender was executed.[90] In private placement adoptions, where there was no surrender to an agency, there also are limitations to any attempted revocation of consent.[91]

It remains to be seen whether the New York courts will fully implement the philosophy as well as the letter of the amended laws. The sentiment that "blood is thicker than water" and the religious doctrine that parents have a natural right to the custody of their children[92] are deep rooted in our culture. Obviously,

---

[88]See Inker: Expanding the rights of children in custody cases, *J. Fam. L., 11:* 129, 1971, and Foster: Revocation of consent to adoption: a covenant running with the child?, *N.Y.L.J.,* Aug. 6, 1971, at 1, cols. 4-5.

[89]N.Y. Soc. Serv. Law § 383(5).

[90]N.Y. Soc. Serv. Law § 384(5).

[91]*Ibid.*

[92]"The rights of parents and guardians under God is inalienable and inviolable because the child belongs primarily and before others to his parents; this natural right has its foundation in the very fact of procreation and involves the right of the parent to feed, clothe and educate his children. . . . These rights involve their corresponding duties which parents may neither evade nor ignore." 6 Augustine,

every thing else being equal, natural parents should prevail in custody contests. But quite often things are not equal and a child's welfare requires that he be awarded to *de facto* or surrogate parents rather than returned to a natural parent. When that is the case, neither sentiment nor religious doctrine, nor the notion that there is a proprietary interest in or a covenant running with the child to the natural parent, should be interposed to the detriment of the child.

This does not mean, however, that a child may be taken from its home and transferred to a more salubrious environment.[93] The natural parents do have prior parental rights unless there has been a forfeiture of such rights by abandonment, neglect, extreme indifference, gross unfitness as parents, or a surrender or placement of the child on a permanent basis.[94] As we shall see in

---

Code of Canon Law 412 (3d ed. 1923). See Comment: Custody and control of children, *Fordham L. Rev.*, 5:460, 1936, reprinted in *Selected Essays on Family Law* (1950) pp. 607, 618, where it is said that "By canon law, by common law, and by statute the natural parents are entitled to the custody of their minor children except when they are unsuitable persons to be entrusted with their care, control and education, or when some special circumstance appears to render such custody inimical to the welfare of the infant." In Lamar v. Harris, 117 Ga. 993, 44 S.E. 866, 868 (1903), the court referred to "those ties which, by the inscrutable province of God, bind men to his own flesh." In Risting v. Sparboe, 179 Iowa 1133, 1136, 162 N.W. 592, 594 (1917), it was "ties of nature, 'bone of their bone and flesh of their flesh.'" In Ex parte Day, 189 Wash. 368, 382, 65 P.2d 1049, 1055 (1937), the court said that "the ties of blood should not be interfered with. . . ." For eulogies on mother love, see Freeland v. Freeland, 92 Wash. 482, 159 P. 698 (1916), and Jenkins v. Jenkins, 173 Wis. 592, 181 N.W. 826 (1921). Compare with the above, Foster: Family law, 1960 annual survey of american family law, *N.Y.U.L. Rev.*, 36:629, 635, 1961: "Perhaps the major impediments to a sound solution of custody issues are the meaningless generality of such principles as 'the best interests of the child' and the persistence of the insensitive sentimentality that 'blood is thicker than water.' Unfortunately, these general propositions too often decide concrete cases. For a wise and just disposition of custody cases, such abstractions need particularization, and standards are needed to spell our amorphous concepts even though more detailed rules are impracticable." For an effort to particularize the general standards, see Oster: Custody proceeding: a study of vague and indefinite standards. *J. Fam. Law*, 5:21, 1965; and Foster and Freed: Child custody. *N.Y.U. L. Rev.*, 39:423, 1964.

---

[93]Such is one of the objectionable features of Painter v. Bannister, 258 Iowa 1390, 140 N.W.2d 152 (1966), cert. denied, 385 U.S. 949 (1966).

[94]See Foster, p. 4 (note 81).

connection with the discussion of *Painter v. Bannister*,[95] a natural parent must be responsible for some event or conduct tantamount to forfeiture before the best interests of the child standard becomes relevant in custody and adoption cases.

Another aspect of the Baby Lenore case which is troublesome is the lack of finality for custodial decrees and the practical inducement that the law provides to the exercise of self-help. In large measure this is due to the inapplicability of the Full Faith and Credit Clause to custody cases[96] and the failure of courts to insist that persons seeking a modification of prior custody awards come into court with *clean hands*.[97] Florida and New York in the past have been most ready to accord a *de novo* hearing for the modification of sister state custody awards, so it is not surprising that they should be at odds again in the Baby Lenore case.[98] To date, the Supreme Court has permitted Florida and New York to withhold full faith and credit from the custody awards of other states.[99]

Mr. Justice Frankfurter, in a well known custody case, took the position that "because the child's welfare is the controlling guide in custody determinations, a custody decree is of an essentially transitory nature."[100] Following the reasoning of prior New York decisions,[101] Mr. Justice Frankfurter eventually concluded that there was no full faith and credit obligation in custody cases, except perhaps regarding prior matters litigated and concluded in the earlier case which had become *res judicata* as distinguished from matters arising since the first decision.[102]

---

[95]Cf. note 93.

[96]See Bodenheimer: Uniform child custody jurisdiction act, *Vand L Rev*, 22: 1207, 1969.

[97]See Foster and Freed: *Law and the Family — New York, vol. 2.* 1967, § 29:35.

[98]See People ex rel. Halvey v. Halvey, 295 N.Y. 836, 66 N.E.2d 851 (1946), aff'd, 330 U.S. 610 (1947); State ex rel. Fox v. Webster, 151 So.2d 14 (Fla. Dist. Ct. App. 1963), cert. denied, 379 U.S. 822 (1964).

[99]*Ibid.*

[100]Kovacs v. Brewer, 356 U.S. 604, 612 (1958).

[101]See Bachman v. Mejias, 1 N.Y.2d 575, 136 N.E.2d 866, 154 N.Y.S.2d 903 (1956), which rejected any full faith and credit obligation in custody cases. See also Berlin v. Berlin, 21 N.Y.2d 371, 235 N.E.2d 109, 288 N.Y.S.2d 44 (1967), cert. denied, 393 U.S. 840 (1968), in which full faith and credit was withheld from 239 Md. 52, 210 A.2d 380 (1965).

[102]See Kovacs v. Brewer, note 100, and Ford v. Ford, 371 U.S. 187 (1962).

In addition to the unfortunate inducement to flight with the child, the lack of finality of custody decisions may be criticized on psychiatric grounds. It has been said that "the first and foremost requirement for the child's health and proper growth is stability, security and continuity."[103] Dr. Andrew Watson contends that stability is "practically the principle element in raising children, especially pre-puberty ones," and that a "child can handle almost anything better than he can handle instability."[104] He also says "poor parental models are easier to adapt to than ever shifting ones."[105] In substance he says that a growing child's need for stability of environment and constancy of affection, especially when subjected to the trauma of a disintegrating home, seems today a well-accepted fact, and concludes that custody decisions once made "should nearly always be permanent and irrevocable."[106] The position of Dr. Watson is amply supported by psychiatric literature and clinical experience.[107] However, unless counsel in the individual case produce expert testimony bearing on psychological factors, and unless the court is willing to listen to opinion evidence, the welfare of the child will not be evaluated in psychological terms.

It is difficult if not impossible to square the prevailing rule as to modifiability of custody orders with the child's need for stability, security, and continuity. Although interstate or international custody disputes have an added dimension of constitutional or international law doctrine, the same psychological dimensions occur in the far more numerous cases where the original order and the attempt at modification occur within one state. It is not uncommon for a divorced couple to seize upon the custody or visitation issue as the focal point for a continuing battle.[108] One well known casebook on Family Law effectively uses a

---

[103]Quoted in Proceedings of Special Committee on Uniform Divorce and Marriage Act, National Conference of Commissioners on Uniform State Laws 98, 101 (Dec. 15-16, 1968).

[104]*Ibid.*

[105]*Ibid.*

[106]*Ibid.* See also Watson: *Psychiatry for Lawyers* (1968).

[107]See Bodenheimer: Uniform child custody jurisdiction act, *Vand L Rev, 22:* 1207, 1209, 1969.

[108]Cf. note 30.

series of hearings and orders for custody and visitation as a motif for its psychoanalytical approach to the general subject of Family Law.[109] However, it does not take much training or psychiatric insight to become aware that children are often pawns in a continuing or renewed struggle between embittered parents.

The practical question is how to safeguard the interests of children in an adversary contest between parents where lawyers representing the parents are obligated to further the interests of their clients. As we shall see, we cannot with confidence rely upon the court or the advocates of parents to highlight the needs and best interests of the children and there is an urgent need that children have independent representation by their own counsel where their placement or welfare is at stake.[110]

Another point which warrants mention is that the psychological and material needs of those the law labels as "minors" differ according to age and maturation. At various stages of development the need for mothering or fathering may be enhanced;[111] with adolescence, individual children may differ with regard to their greater need for one or the other parent.[112] To some extent

---

[109]*Ibid.*

[110]See Speca and Wehrman: Protecting the rights of children in divorce cases in Missouri, U.M.K.C.L. Rev., *38*:1, 1969; and Foster and Freed: A bill of rights for children, *N.Y.L.J.*, July 28, 1972, at 1, cols. 4-5.

[111]See Patton: *Growth Failure in Maternal Deprivation* (1963), p. 38. See also, Davie, Butler, and Goldstein: *From Birth to Seven* (1972), Second Report of the English National Child Development Survey.

[112]It generally is agreed that for normal development a child needs both a mother and father model and that the loss of either is damaging. Deprivation of a mother is most serious for infants; a boy needs a father or father figure for his normal development. Loss of security and feelings of rejection are apt to occur when parents are separated by divorce. See Gardner: Separation of the parents and the emotional life, *Mental Hygiene, 40*:53-54, 1956, where it is suggested that substantial visitation with the non-custodial parent may help but that unless the visits are lengthy they can result in increased confusion for the child. There must be time enough in order to maintain a meaningful relationship. See also Wylie and Delgado: A pattern of mother-son relationships involving the absence of the father, *J of Orthopsychiatry, 29*:644, 1959. Usually, it is desirable that children maintain contacts with their father even though their mother remarries and they acquire a stepfather. See Simon: *Stepchild in the Family,* (1964), p. 116. Some of the problems of child adjustment to parental divorce are discussed in Note, *J Fam Law, 8*:58, 59-62, 1968. See also, Comment: Custody and control of children,

the law reflects the developmental needs of children, although often in a haphazard fashion. There is a clear tendency to award infants to the mother and to give her custody of daughters.[113]

Fordham L Rev., 5:460, 1936, reprinted in A.A.L.S., Selected Essays on Family Law, (1950), p. 607; White House Conference on Child Health and Protection, section IV (1930), where it is stated that the child's conflicting loyalties, varying with the calendar, deprive him of a sense of security which is essential to normal development. Of general interest are Despert: *Children of Divorce* (1962); Ackerman: *The Psychodynamics of Family Life* (1958); *Neurotic Interaction in Marriage, The Psychoanalytic Study of the Family* (1954) (Eisenstein ed. 1956); Fluegel, Levy and Monroe: *The Happy Family* (1938); and Plant: The psychiatrist views children of divorced parents, *Law & Contemp Prob,* 1944, 807.

See Note, Divided custody of children after their parents divorce, *J Fam Law, 8:58,* 1968, where it is pointed out that Jupiter's division of custody of Prosperina between a custodian in hell and another on earth "has been cited as one of the few instances of divided custody in antiquity, when society's powers of investigation were less effective and there generally was less concern for children." The author says that at the beginning of the twentieth century there was almost a total judicial prohibition of divided custody. Only one state, North Carolina, specifically forbids divided custody by statute. See N.C. Gen. Stat. § 50-13 (1953). Louisiana courts categorically disallow such awards. See Bush v. Bush, 163 So.2d 858, 860 (La. 1964). Usually it is stated that divided custody is undesirable and will not be approved except under exceptional circumstances. See Bronner v. Bronner, 278 S.W.2d 530 (Tex. Civ. App. 1954). One factor that may lead to divided custody is the need of a small son to know and have the companionship of his father. See Mason v. Zolnosky, 103 N.W.2d 752 (Iowa 1960). Another factor is the agreement parents have made for divided custody. See Flanagan v. Flanagan, 247 P.2d 212 (Ore. 1952). Of course, it is a condition precedent to divided custody that both parents be "fit" parents. Moreover, if divided custody proves harmful to the child, it will be terminated and exclusive custody will be awarded to one parent, perhaps with visitation rights to the other. See Husten v. Husten, 122 N.W.2d 892 (Iowa 1963), and Dunn v. Dunn, 217 S.W.2d 124 (Tex. Civ. App. 1949).

[113]It has been estimated that the mother prevails ninety percent of the time in custody disputes with the father, at least where infants are involved. See Drinan: The rights of children in modern American family life, *J Fam Law,* 2:101-102, 1962. Another estimate is that she wins four-fifths of all custody cases. See Jacobson: *American Marriage and Divorce* (1959), p. 131. Favoritism for the mother occurs even though statutes such as New York's Dom. Rel. Law § 70 provide ". . . there shall be no *prima facie* right to the custody of the child in either parent, but the court shall determine solely what is for the best interests of the child . . ."

The judicial preference for awarding young children to their mother is supported not only by experience but by a vast literature in the area of child psychology and psychiatry. With reference to infants, some of the most influential

The father has his best chance to prevail in a custody dispute with the mother where teen age sons are the subject of dispute,[114] although otherwise the odds are all in her favor. Moreover, courts are reluctant to separate siblings, if such can be avoided, hence sons as well as daughters usually will be awarded to the mother where she seeks custody of all of the children.[115] Within these

studies have been those of Rene Spitz: Hospitalism, an inquiry into the genesis of psychiatric conditions in early childhood, *The Psychoanalytic Study of the Child*, *Vol. I*, New York, International Universities Press, (1945). The writings on child development by Arnold Gesell are among the best known contributions in this field. His book *The First Five Years of Life* appeared in 1940, and he was co-author of the study *The Child From Five to Ten* that appeared in 1946, and *Youth, The Years From Ten to Sixteen* (1956). The series on child psychiatry published by the Group for the Advancement of Psychiatry also are significant. Finch's *Fundamentals of Child Psychiatry* (1960) is helpful for the legal profession. A classic is Erikson's *Childhood and Society* (2 ed. 1963). Also of special interest to the lawyer are English and Foster: *Fathers Are Parents Too* (1951); English and Finch, *Emotional Problems of Growing Up* (1951); Fleugel, Levy and Monroe: *The Happy Family* (1938); Benedek: The psychosomatic implications of primary unit: mother-child. *Amer. J. of Orthopsychiatry*, 19:642, 1949; and Jones: *Raising Your Child in a Fatherless Home* (1963).

[114]According to psychological theory boys learn to be masculine through identification with their fathers and the lack of a father, or his prolonged absence, especially during a critical stage such as the oedipal period, causes problems with sex-role identification, delinquency, and mental disturbances characterized by high anxiety. Stolz, in his book entitled *Father Relations of War-Born Children* (1954), found that father-separated boys not only showed more feminine fantasy behavior, but also were more feminine in their overt behavior. However, it should be noted that other males, including siblings and peers, may serve as role-models in child development. Moreover, many writers agree that an inadequate father may be the equivalent to no father, and it is clear that the absence of a father is no guarantee of maladjustment. Between the ages of six months and seven years the effects of permanent separation from a parent seem to be at their worst. See Skard: Maternal deprivation: the research and its implications, *J Marr & Fam*, 27:333, 1965. Finally, it also is generally agreed that permanent removal from parents to an institutional setting is very often, although not always, conducive to intellectual, psychological, and social deficits. For a decision awarding custody of two young children to the father, without any finding that the mother was unfit or immoral, see Johnson v. Johnson, 7 Utah2d 263, 323 P.2d 16 (1958), and for a bitter criticism of the propensity to award custody to the mother, see Metz: *Divorce and Custody for Men* (1968).

[115]See Brashear v. Brashear, 71 Idaho 158, 228 P.2d 243 (1951), but compare Randolph v. Randolph, 146 Fla. 491, 1 So.2d 480 (1941), commented upon in B.U.L. Rev. *21*:732, 1941. See also Penn v. Abell, 173 S.W.2d 483 (Tex. Civ. App. 1943) (adopted brothers), and Gardner v. Pettit, 192 So.2d 696 (Miss. 1967).

limitations, courts may be willing to listen to psychiatric testimony concerning the immediate needs of a particular child at a
particular stage of development. The stated preference of the
teenage child as to custody or visitation also may be a factor to be
considered by the court.

The recommendation that counsel offer and that courts admit
expert testimony concerning the dynamics of inter-relationships
and the psychological aspects of custody disputes does not imply
that courts should forsake their traditional fact finding role.
Painter v. Bannister,[116] previously referred to, illustrates the
problem of psychological testimony gone wild and the inappropriate application of a sound rule to the wrong fact situation. In
this Iowa case, as may be recalled, the court decided that four
year old Mark's welfare would be better served by remaining on
an Iowa farm with elderly maternal grandparents than by return-
ing him to his father and new stepmother who were living in
what was described as the *Bohemian atmosphere* of the San Fran-
cisco Bay Area.

The major error in the Iowa decision is that there was no
cause to get into an invidious comparison of rural Iowa and the
Golden Gate. Mark had been temporarily placed by the distraught father with the grandparents, following the tragic death
of the mother and baby sister in a car accident, on the express
understanding that Mark would be returned as soon as the father
re-established a home. There was no relinquishment nor abandonment by the father. Under these circumstances, to award legal
custody to the grandparents was the equivalent of taking a child
from a lower income home in order to place him with a more af-
fluent couple who could offer greater material advantages. There
was no basis for the operation of the so-called best interests rule.
As we have said, that rule should not come into play until some
behavior or event has occurred which is tantamount to a relinquishment of parental rights. The Iowa court correctly rejected
the overwhelming weight of older legal authority that in most
cases automatically applies an automatic preference for the natu-

---

[116]140 N.W.2d 152 (Iowa 1966), cert. denied, 385 U.S. 949 (1966). The father
who lost custody wrote a book entitled *Mark, I Love You* (1967), and eventually
the maternal grandparents returned Mark to him.

ral parent,[117] but in so doing it automatically applied the best interests rule in the wrong fact situation.

The *Painter* case also involved a problem of misapplied psychology. At the trial expert testimony of a competent child psychologist was introduced in behalf of the grandparents. He was the only expert witness. The transcript shows that he was permitted to ramble without interruption or objection and that there was no meaningful cross-examination. Admittedly, he had not seen the father. A great deal of his testimony was the grossest kind of speculation and many of the conclusions he arrived at were questionable or controversial from the standpoint of child psychology.[118] The trial judge considered but rejected the expert testimony but the appellate court seized upon it to bolster its decision that Mark should remain with the grandparents.

Thus we see that although there is an urgent need for competent expert testimony in child custody cases it also is essential that there be a balanced presentation of opinion and that conclusions be subjected to the search of incisive cross-examination. The *psychological* well-being of the child should be the focal point where the best interests rule comes into play and there should be concern over his "affection relationship" and his personality development, but the ultimate decision must be that of a court which insists upon compiling all the facts, psychological and otherwise.

Our conclusion with reference to the principle that a child is entitled to receive parental love and affection, discipline and guidance, and to grow to maturity in a home environment which enables him to develop into a mature and responsible adult, is that this moral principle has received but limited legal sanction. The courts assume jurisdiction where a child is abused or abandoned, or becomes incorrigible or a person in need of supervision, but only in flagrant cases. In disputes as to custody or

---

[117]See Foster and Freed: Child custody, *NYUL Rev, 37:*423, 615, 1964.

[118]For example, the child psychologist testified that it would be harmful to take Mark away from the grandparents, even though he also testified that Mark had shown capacity to adjust to changes in custody. It would be as logical to say that the fears the psychologist expressed were not consistent with Mark's past record of adaptability.

placement, the above moral principle may be relevant under the rubric of the *best interests of the child* standard and it is in such cases that psychiatric and psychological evidence may have its greatest impact. To date, however, it would be hyperbole to claim that the moral principle has evolved into a recognized legal norm.

CHAPTER FOUR

TO BE SUPPORTED, MAINTAINED, AND EDUCATED

to the best of parental ability, in return for which
he has the moral duty to honor his father and
mother.

THE CHILD'S RIGHT TO SUPPORT, maintenance, and education usually has been expressed in terms of the father's duty to provide the same. Blackstone enumerated three duties owed by parents to a child, namely to provide maintenance, protection, and education.[119] Chancellor Kent referred only to the duty to maintain and the duty to educate.[120]

The tragedy, however, is that these parental duties or rights of children, until relatively recently, were not backed up by effective legal sanctions. In England, it was up to the ecclesiastical courts or the clergy to persuade a devout believer, under pain of penance, to perform his parental duty.[121] Common law remedies were ineffectual or non-existent. However, under the poor laws a parish might recoup for handouts doled out to abandoned families.[122] There was, moreover, the possibility of an uncertain action by creditors to recover for the price of necessities given to

---

[119]Blackstone's Commentaries 194 (Gavit Ed. 1941). Maintenance is the obligation to provide for the offspring; protection is not defined except as to natural duty; education is said to be of great importance but it is noted that there was no legal sanction. See Speca and Wehrman: Protecting the rights of children in divorce cases in Missouri, *U.M.K.C. L. Rev.*, 38:1, 1969.

[120]Kent: *Commentaries on American Law*, (Brownes ed. 1894), pp. 260-267.

[121]In addition, chancery imposed a quasi-contractual duty to support children which in some states became a matter of equity. See Greenspan v. Slate, 12 N.J. 426, 97 A.2d 390 (1953).

[122]The Elizabethan Poor Laws of the early seventeenth century (43 Eliz. I, c. 2) authorized such actions See Mortimore v. Wright, 6 Mees. & W. 482 (1840), and Shelton v. Springett, 11 C.B. 452 (1851).

the family.[123] None of these sanctions proved effective and it was relatively easy for an errant father to disappear or go to sea in order to avoid his familial obligations.

Today most states have multiple actions and remedies to enforce the child support obligation, ranging from criminal, quasi-criminal, to civil actions.[124] The Uniform Reciprocal Enforcement of Support Act has been a most important statute in child support cases and permits the deserted family to initiate an action for support at home and to have the father brought before the court where he is found and subjected to the personal jurisdiction and power of that court.[125] The responding state may enter and enforce the support order so that there is no need to extradite the father and bring him back to the initiating state.

Despite alternative remedies and the Uniform Act, a substantial percentage of support orders are not paid at all or are not paid on time.[126] The reasons for noncompliance with support orders are both economic and psychological. Support orders may be unrealistic in amount and courts may fail to take into account the additional expenses that accrue when the family is broken up and the father maintains a separate home, or acquires a second

---

[123]Unlike the situation where the wife was permitted to pledge her husband's credit for necessaries, a child had no such privilege, except where there was express or implied authorization from the father according to agency principles. Otherwise, neither the child nor any creditor who had provided him with necessaries had any cause of action against the parent. An infant could not sue a parent with or without a guardian *ad litem.* No action in assumpsit was maintainable. However, in the nineteenth century it was held that a wife who was justifiably living apart from her husband due to his misconduct and having legal custody of the children could pledge her husband's credit and he was liable for necessaries received by the wife, including clothes for the child. See Bazeley v. Forder, [1868] L.R. 3 Q.B. 559.

[124]See Foster: Dependent children and the law, *U Pitt L Rev, 18:*579, 1957.

[125]For a full discussion of the URESA and a citation of cases, see Brockelbank and Infausto: *Interstate Enforcement of Family Support* (2d ed. 1971).

[126]One of the few accurate studies is that by Fred. H. Steininger: Study of Divorce and Support Orders in Lake County Indiana, 1956-1957, submitted to the Lake County Welfare Board, which shows that there were arrearages in eighty-nine percent of the cases and that no payments were ever made in forty-seven percent of the cases, even though the payments were ordered to be made directly to the court.

family.[127] More important, however, is the manner in which support cases are processed in many metropolitan centers. Typically, an overburdened court rushes through support hearings and on an *ad hoc* basis sets an amount for support.[128] The embittered father may not be permitted to explain his side of the family controversy and he leaves the courtroom bound and determined not to pay if he can avoid it. To place him in jail for contempt may be unrealistic because then he is cut off from all earnings.

There are a few jurisdictions where support orders generally are complied with and payments are made on time. The requirement that support payments be made to the court rather than to the estranged wife has some efficacy where there is an immediate follow up on arrearages.[129] Most effective, however, is the simple technique of calling the obligor to an informal pretrial conference at which he is permitted to air his side of the family difficulty and to suggest an amount that he is willing to pay.[130] If the figure is reasonable, it may be approved by the court. Since the obligor participated in arriving at the agreed upon amount and had a chance to air his grievances, he usually views the support order as a moral obligation. In two counties in Pennsylvania where this practice is in effect, over ninety percent of support orders were compiled with on time, and in the remaining cases, frequently the obligor had suffered a reduction in income or had some excuse for noncompliance.[131]

Although there is general agreement that there should be effective legal machinery to enforce the support duty the record on collection is a poor one.[132] There may be less agreement as to the extent of the duty to support where the child is illegitimate. In the past, the laws of some states have discriminated against illegit-

---

[127]See Foster, note 124. It should be noted, however, that many courts reckon how much is needed for the basic care of the man, and then set the amount of wife or child support accordingly. A rough rule of thumb, subject to many exceptions, is that support for a wife should be about one-third of the man's net income, and where there are children it may go up to half his net income.

[128]See Foster, note 124.

[129]For example, Detroit, Wayne County, Michigan has such a system.

[130]See Foster, note 124.

[131]*Ibid.*

[132]See note 126.

imate children as compared with legitimate offspring.[133] Recent Supreme Court decisions have held that such discrimination is unconstitutional, although the Court also has held that a state may distinguish between legitimate and illegitimate children in its inheritance laws.[134] For the purposes of this discussion it is sufficient to note that historically there has been a lesser duty of support in the case of illegitimate children but that current constitutional theory requires equal treatment in that regard.[135]

The principle of support as set forth above imposes the support obligation equally on both parents. The parental duty should be joint and several, or to put it differently, the measure of the mutual duty is joint ability, and each parent has the duty to contribute to the extent of his or her respective resources. If the mother has greater resources or income, under this principle, she could be called upon to contribute more than the father to the children's support, maintenance, and education. The premise is that the parents should be treated equally and without sex discrimination. Establishment of a mutual obligation for child support would constitute a departure from the law of most if not all states where typically the father has the primary and the mother only a secondary duty. When the duty cannot be enforced against the father, the principles of the equal rights for women move-

---

[133]Idaho and Texas have been unique in not providing for support actions against the fathers of illegitimate children. Missouri, which formerly made such a discrimination, held its statutes unconstitutional in R. v. R., 431 S.W.2d 152 (Mo. 1968). Moreover, some states cut off the natural father's support duty at an earlier age where his child is illegitimate and some states place a ceiling on the amount he may be ordered to pay. For example, see Fla. Stat. Ann. (West Supp. 1960) § 742.031.

[134]See Gomez v. Perez, 93 S.ct. 872 (1973). See also Levy v. Louisiana, 391 U.S. 68 (1968), and Glona v. American Guarantee Co., 391 U.S. 73 (1968), holding that illegitimate dependents must be treated the same as legitimate dependent children under wrongful death acts. However, in Labine v. Vincent, 401 U.S. 532 (1971), it was held that for inheritance purposes a state may discriminate between legitimate and illegitimate children. Stanley v. Illinois, 405 U.S. 645 (1972), however held that a putative father had standing and was entitled to a hearing as to his paternal fitness before his children might be taken from him and made wards of the state.

[135]See Krause: Legitimate and illegitimate offspring of Levy v. Louisiana, *U Chic L Rev, 36*:338, 1960; and Krause: Equal protection for the illegitimate. *Mich L Rev, 65*:477, 1967.

ment and canons of equal protection require that parents be placed on a parity with regard to child support.[136] However, imposition of such a joint duty should be conditioned upon a fair system of marital property law that treats the parties as equal partners with regard to family assets accumulated during the marriage.[137]

It is only fair that something in return be given for the sometimes onerous duty of child support. We have phrased that reciprocal duty in the traditional terms of "honor thy father and mother." It has been labeled as a moral duty because of the practical difficulties that arise from the application of legal sanctions.

It should be noted, however, that under the juvenile court laws of most states incorrigibles or persons in need of supervision (PINS) or the *stubborn child* may be hauled before a juvenile court by the parents.[138] In extreme situations, the pre-delinquent or non-delinquent child may be taken from the home.[139] Usually, however, child and family counseling is the approved technique. Child guidance centers in urban areas may provide similar services. The point is that counseling is the approved procedure and the threat of juvenile court adjudication with an accompanying stigmatic label may be counter-productive. Unless a juvenile court has a competent professional staff, resort to its procedures may merely aggravate the family situation.

There also is the situation where a minor disobeys parental instructions and litigation develops between parent and child. A relatively recent New York case involved a suit for child support brought against the father by his twenty year old daughter who

---

[136]Kanowitz: *Women and the Law* (1969), p. 69, concedes that "the universal rule is that the primary obligation to provide financial support to the family rests on the husband." Obviously, an equal rights amendment would make that rule discriminatory.

[137]In those common law property states where a court is not given discretion to distribute property upon divorce, no matter how title is held, the marital property system may be such that it would be unfair to impose an equal duty of support upon the wife. See Foster and Freed, Marital property reform: partnership of co-equals?, *NYLJ*, *169*:43, 57, 82, March 5, 23, and April 27, 1973.

[138]See note 60.

[139]*Ibid.*

was attending college away from home.[140] The daughter had nearly flunked out of school and had been involved to some extent with the drug scene. The father who had been paying all her expenses and who had provided her with a car, instructed the daughter to live in the college dormitory. Some months later he learned that she had taken an apartment with another female. He demanded that she return to the dormitory or enroll in school in New York where he could keep his eye on her. She refused, and when he cut off her allowance, the daughter sued for child support, including educational expenses. At the trial the father, who was a prominent attorney, behaved in authoritarian fashion and told the court it had no authority to tell him how to treat his daughter. He also made offensive and insulting remarks about the daughter. The trial judge issued an order requiring the father to pay back payments of the allowance and to pay such allowance in the future until the daughter reached majority. The appellate court in New York overruled this decision, holding that a parent might impose reasonable conditions in such circumstances and if the child disobeyed, he might terminate support.[141] The notion was that rebellious children should not have it both ways, especially where they are regarded as "rebels without a cause."

The above case presents a number of difficult problems. Obviously, courts should be wary of such internecine conflicts, else they will be called upon to write budgets and codes of behavior for the family.[142] Moreover, counseling rather than litigation seems to be the more reasonable approach to such problems. Both father and daughter were further embittered by their courtroom experience. It was their relationship which warranted and needed attention and a court decision in terms of reciprocal duty did nothing to heal the breach.

For the most part, then, the moral duty to honor parents cannot be effectively implemented by the law. Respect is something

---

[140]Roe v. Doe, 36 App. Div. 2d 162, 318 N.Y.S.2d 973 (1971).

[141]*Ibid.*

[142]Compare McGuire v. McGuire, 157 Neb. 226, 59 N.W.2d 336 (1953), which refused to award a wife support where she was still living with a miserly husband.

which must be earned and which cannot be imposed from above. Moreover, one of the best ways to earn respect is to give it to others. In other words, if children are treated as persons, ordinarily they will honor their parents.

CHAPTER FIVE

TO RECEIVE FAIR TREATMENT

from all in authority and to
be heard and listened to.

THE DECISION in Gault[143] established that minors before a juvenile court have a constitutional right to fair treatment and that where delinquency is charged the rudiments of a fair trial must be observed, at least at the adjudicatory stage of the proceedings. The Supreme Court did not hold that all of the canons of criminal due process must be applied, nor did it hold them to be mandatory at the intake or dispositional stages of a juvenile court proceeding.[144] However, the tenor of the majority opinion, as well as its rationale, support the general proposition that juveniles are constitutionally entitled to fair treatment by police and juvenile authorities, and that where there is a departure from ordinary due process, there must be justification for the deviance.[145] There is a danger, however, that long standing custom or a tradition of informality may be accepted as justification.[146]

There also is the more general problem of justification for a separate system for processing juvenile cases. The premise behind the juvenile court movement is that minors below a stipulated age will be removed from criminal procedure in order to provide individualized rehabilitative treatment. Officially, punishment or

---

[143]In re Gualt, 387 U.S. 1 (1967).

[144]See Foster: Notice and "fair procedure:" revolution or simple revision?, printed in *ICLE, Gault: What now for the juvenile court?*, 1968, p. 51; and Dorsen and Rezneck: In re Gault and the future of juvenile law, *Fam Law Q, 1*:1, 1967.

[145]Ibid. See also, Allen: *The Borderland of Criminal Justice* (1964), and Report by the President's Commission on Law Enforcement and Administration of Justice, Task Force on Juvenile Justice, "Juvenile Delinquency and Youth Crime" (1967), for a detailed analysis of the juvenile court system.

[146]McKeiver v. Pennsylvania, 403 U.S. 528 (1971), held that there was no constitutional right to a jury trial in juvenile court.

retribution was disavowed and since such was not an objective it followed that a relaxation of criminal procedures was not only permissible but desirable.[147] It did not occur to the sponsors of the juvenile court movement that minors were exchanging their birthright for a mess of pottage and might receive what Justice Fortes described as the *worst of both worlds*.[148] In order to provide treatment rather than punishment, the system required ample resources of personnel, program, and plant.[149] Very few if any juvenile courts were blessed with such resources and typically the judge was faced with a Hobson's choice between undesirable alternatives. Juvenile institutions were more often than not plagued with the vices and inadequacies of their adult counterparts,[150] probation officers were over-burdened with caseloads,[151] and the home environment of the minor was conducive to delinquency.[152] The potential for treatment and rehabilitation which the system envisionaged simply was not realized, and, unprotected by the rules of criminal justice, juveniles were caught up in a system which from their point of view was both unjust and hypocritical.

Most important, neither the law nor those administering it took into account the workings of the system from the child's

---

[147]For example, see Application of Gault, 99 Ariz. 181, 407 P.2d 760 (1965), and In re Holmes, 379 Pa. 599, 109 A.2d 523 (1954), cert. denied, 348 U.S. 973 (1954), and especially the dissenting opinion by Justice Musmanno.

[148]Kent v. United States, 383 U.S. 541, 556 (1966).

[149]See Alexander: Constitutional rights in the juvenile court, in *Justice for the Child* (Rosenheim ed.), (1962), p. 82.

[150]See Rubin: Children as victims of institutionalization, *Child Welfare, 60:6*, 1972, and for a documented study, see the report of the Committee on Health Services Inside and Outside the Family Court in New York City, entitled "Juvenile Justice Confounded: Pretentions and Realities in Treatment Services."

[151]"One thing is certain: most probation officers see their probationers infrequently and briefly. In the largest population centers . . . an average of once a month. In some big cities . . . only every three months or even less frequently. . . . In many juvenile courts the probation officer has such a large caseload that his contacts with the child are so hurried and infrequent as to be meaningless." Forer: *No One Will Lissen* (1970), p. 176.

[152]His [the judge's] only alternatives are to return the girl to what is evidently an impossible home situation or to hold her in jail. There are no nonpunitive shelters for boys or girls of this age." *Ibid*, p. 227.

viewpoint. *Roberts v. State*,[153] is an early and extreme example. In that case the Nebraska court affirmed commitment of a sixteen year old boy to an industrial school for an indeterminate sentence (possibly until age twenty-one) because he swore at a church meeting of young people. The penalty for blasphemy for an adult was a fine of twenty-five cents to a dollar. The court said: "Our industrial school is not a place of punishment nor is it in any sense a prison, no more than our public schools . . . It is a place of education, reformation, refinement, and culture. It is a beneficent provision for the uplift of boys who by reason of their surroundings are deprived of an educational and moral training which are so essential to their well-being and good citizenship . . . The action of the court . . . is to avoid a *conviction* and change the prospective punishment into a blessing." The facts of the *Gault* case were similarly outrageous from young Gerald Gault's point of view,[154] and a recent study of the juvenile court in Philadelphia convincingly shows that conditions have improved but little since that landmark decision. [155]

It is doubtful that genuine reformation may be had if the system is unfair or if an individual juvenile is unfairly treated by those in authority. The high recidivism rate of juvenile and adult offenders is indicative of both the failure of the supposed rehabilitation process and the bitterness engendered by unfair treatment. In a sense, individualized treatment perforce is counter-productive because of the fact or appearance of discrimination. From the standpoint of the juvenile offender, an indeterminate sentence or institutionalization for a longer period of time than that for an adult convicted of a comparable offense is *per se* dis-

---

[153]82 Neb. 651, 118 N.W. 674 (1908).

[154]Fifteen-year-old Gerald Gault was picked up and taken to the police station while his parents were at work. No notice or specification of charges were given to him or his parents. He was not represented by counsel until after the adjudication. No record of a hearing was made; there was no confrontation of witnesses against him; and hearsay statements were accepted. He received an indeterminate sentence (possible confinement until he was 21) for allegedly having made a "lewd phone call," a misdemeanor for which an adult (who received due process of law) might be fined from five to fifty dollars or might be sentenced to serve up to two months in jail.

[155]Forer: *No One Will Lissen* (1971).

criminatory and justification in terms of rehabilitation is absurd. Bitterness and cynicism are not the products of the ordinary defense mechanism of rationalization but are based upon a legitimate grievance.

As is true in the case of the indeterminate sentence of so-called sex psychopaths, where the logic of behavioral science failed to reckon with political practicality,[156] the juvenile court movement likewise was victimized by political logistics. Legislatures and the public failed to deliver the financial support that is needed for the implementation of behavioral theory. Personnel, plant, and program, uniformly were inadequate to the commitment. It is understandable that the whole system has come under attack and that some competent observers call for its abolition,[157] while others hopefully seek substantial reform that legislatures are reluctant to provide.[158] Benign neglect has triggered off skepticism as to the rehabilitative ideal and the realities of the American corrective system. The two may be utterly incompatible when we remember the dismal record of legislative and public support.

Constitutional issues aside, it is unfair from the juvenile's point of view that the juvenile court process may deny him the adult privilege against self-incrimination, the right to notice, right to counsel, the right to confrontation, and other elements of essential fairness on the theory that he is receiving help rather than punishment. Who needs such help? But the right to fair treatment is not limited to the forensic area. Kangaroo courts may be set up at home or school. Arbitrary or officious behavior by adults is a common phenomenon experienced by many children. Many adults fail to appreciate that fair procedure and rules are essential for a just determination of controversies and that the lawyer's *red tape* is not hypertechnicality but a reasoned approach to fact-finding when facts are disputed.[159] Guilt by association, a

---

[156]See Tenny: Sex, sanity, and stupidity in Massachusetts, *BU L Rev, 42:1,* 1962; Robitscher: Statutes, law enforcement, and the judicial process, in Resnik and Wolfgang: *Sexual Behavior: Social, Clinical and Legal Aspects* (1972).

[157]Forer, note 155. See also Rubin: Children as victims of institutionalization, *Child Welfare, 60:6,* 1972.

[158]See Midonick: *Children, Parents and the Courts,* (1972).

[159]See Foster: Social work, the law, and social action, in *Social Casework,* July 1964, p. 383.

presumption of guilt, and the denial of an opportunity to be heard, or to confront and refute, all too often are the indicia of lay procedure. To the lawyer there is a two-fold objection to such inquisitorial methods: first, it is not calculated to discover the truth; and, second, it constitutes an affront to human dignity. Unfair procedure is not to be forgiven merely because the penalty is relatively slight, for any sanction is unduly severe if the procedure is unfair. Moreover, it is self-defeating, because it will be resented as unjust.

One of the most frequent complaints of children is that grownups won't listen.[160] Admittedly, it takes patience to be a good listener, and it is difficult to cultivate the art, especially if one regards the speaker as an intellectual inferior or as immature. To the extent that the generation gap is a communications problem, adult inability to listen is a major source of difficulty.

The tendency of youths and adults to be on different wave lengths extends beyond intra-family communications. It is conspicuous in our schools, churches, mass media, and wherever there are attempts at communication between different age groups. Unfortunately, stereotypes of the young and the old block the free exchange of ideas and each side may merely seek to confirm preconceptions. Even where they are heard, youth may not be listened to.

As persons, children deserve a better audience than they ordinarily receive, and they are entitled to reasoned argument in lieu of ultimatims. Understanding is promoted, if not achieved, when reasons are given for decisions.

The right to be heard includes the right to have standing in legal proceedings to assert one's claim of interest. It is anomalous that under the procedure of most states children are unrepresent-

---

[160]"When a child requests a reason or explanation concerning a particular restriction, at least two responses are open to a parent. On the one hand, the parent may fulfill the request and demand compliance; on the other, the parent may ignore the child's inquiry. From the child's perspective, this is essentially the difference between the expression of legitimate and coercive power." Elder: Parental power legitimation and its effect on the adolescent, reprinted in Goldstein and Katz, *The Family and the Law* (1965), p. 980. See also, Forer: *No One Will Lissen* (1971).

ed when their parents seek a divorce.[161] The major issue in dispute may be custody and visitation rights, and in a practical sense the children may be the real parties in interest where their placement is at stake. Nonetheless, courts traditionally have assumed that only the parents need to be represented by counsel and that the child's preference is a minor factor to be considered in determining custody.[162] This may be due to mere habit because unless specific statutes or court rules prohibit, there is inherent power in the divorce court to appoint counsel to represent children and to grant leave for them to intervene.[163]

In Wisconsin, pursuant to statute and court decision,[164] a guardian *ad litem* may be appointed to represent minor children when their parents seek divorce. The guardian may introduce evidence, have investigations made, and cross-examine witnesses. Moreover, a so-called "Bill of Rights of Children in Divorce Actions" is handed to parents before trial in order to remind them of their parental obligations.

States which have recently reformed their divorce law and procedure, such as California, Iowa, New York, and Oregon, have enacted various devices in an effort to safeguard the interests of children.[165] In addition, several states require welfare department or probation staff investigations when custody is disputed,[166] and

---

[161]See Speca and Wehrman: Protecting the rights of children in divorce cases in Missouri, *UMKC L Rev, 38:*1, 1969.

[162]See People v. Glendening, 259 App. Div. 384, 19 N.Y.S. 693 (1940), but compare Smith v. Smith, 15 Utah 2d 36, 386 P.2d 900 (1963) (construing Utah statute).

[163]See Speca and Wehrman, note 161. See also Wendland v. Wendland, 29 Wis. 2d 145, 138 N.W.2d 185 (1965); Barth v. Barth, 12 Ohio Misc. 141, 225 N.E.2d 866 (1967); and Zinni v. Zinni, 238 A.2d 373 (R.I. 1968).

[164]Wendland v. Wendland, note 163. See also Wis. Stat. Ch. 245.001(2), and Ch. 247.15(1) (Supp. 1971-72); and Hansen: The role and rights of children in divorce actions, *J Fam Law, 6:*1, 1966.

[165]For example see New York Dom. Rel. Law § 215-c which authorizes the appointment of a guardian to represent children in divorce cases. Such authority has been but rarely utilized.

[166]In Colorado and certain counties in Texas such reports are mandatory. See 10 Colo. Rev. Stat. Ann. Ch. 46-1-5 (supp. 1967), and Ver. Ann. Civ. Stat. Tex. art. 2338-18 § 13 (1967). See also Connolly: Divorce proctors, *BU L Rev, 34:*1, 1954; and Cox: The divorce proctor, *Tenn L Rev 33:*439, 1966.

still others require that the district attorney or some other public official be notified when the parties seeking divorce have children under a certain age.[167] In Michigan, for example, the prosecuting attorney is directed by statute to appear at the hearing and to introduce evidence opposing the divorce if the interests of the children and the public good so require.[168]

Assuming that the American adversary system is likely to survive, this matter of independent representation by counsel, so that children have their own lawyer when their placement or welfare is at stake, may be the most significant and practical device for the presentation of their point of view. Proponents of the adversary process should not object to making the system functional so that all interests may be heard.

Children have individual interests apart from and sometimes in conflict with parental or societal interests. Their interests are entitled to be heard and that can be done only through independent representation. Counsel for either parent owes a paramount duty to his client and cannot and should not be relied upon to promote the best interests of children unless they coincide with those of his client. Moreover, busy courts faced with a backlog of cases do not have the time or usually the inclination to sort out the evidence and the issues from the child's point of view.

Placement of the child, whether the issue arises in a custody, adoption, or neglect proceeding, is a matter of crucial importance to him. Quite literally, his life and future are at stake. The consequences of an ill-advised placement may be as traumatic or dire as commitment to an institution. The same reasons that justify the extension of due process principles to delinquency proceedings also apply to the placement issue and in truth the need for independent counsel may be even greater because only about

---

[167]This requirement exists in Delaware, the District of Columbia, Georgia, Hawaii, Indiana, Kentucky, Massachusetts, Michigan, Nebraska, Washington, West Virginia, Wisconsin, and Wyoming. See Clark: Law of domestic relations, 1968 p 381, for a citation of statutes.

[168]Mich. Stat. Ann. § 25.121 (1969). See also Harv. Legis., 5:563, 1968, which contains a "Divorce Reform Act" and the concept that children whose parents seek divorce are parties to the action who should be represented by counsel so that their interests will be protected.

twenty percent of juveniles found to be delinquents are institutionalized.[169]

In the past, many if not most courts have been insensitive to
the conflict of interests inherent in traditional procedures where
a child's placement is at issue and have perceived no need for independent counsel. In large measure, this may be due to tradition, a desire to conserve time or a propensity to duck difficult
issues, or because lawyers usually have not pressed the interests of
children *qua* children. There also is a pervasive paternalism derived from the feudal status of children and the concept that children are not people, but the objects of paternal rights.

It may be contended that it would delay litigation and that it
would be too expensive if there were a mandatory rule that children be represented by independent counsel wherever their welfare or placement were at issue. This objection overlooks the fact
that *Gault* already requires such independent representation in
delinquency cases and that a system or panel of law guardians
could extend representation to other cases. Moreover, there is a
fresh crop of young lawyers at hand who may be eager to serve
the interests of children and dispensation might be granted to
law students to appear as counsel for children in appropriate
cases. The child should have his day in court, and if he is to
be listened to, he will need a lawyer. In a litigious and conten-
tious society, youth needs its own advocate or it will not be heard.

The need for independent representation may be greatly increased by the current liberalization of divorce laws and the
adoption of non-fault grounds for divorce. Divorce reform in California, Colorado, and Kentucky,[170] and legislation such as the

---

[169]Judge Midonick (note 138 at 82) reports that the Family Court of New York
City handles about nine thousand delinquency and seven thousand PINS cases a
year, but only forty to fifty cases each year involving murder, first-degree
rape, or first-degree arson. The dismissal rate on delinquency cases is about forty
percent. *Ibid.*, p. 98. Of the cases proceeding to disposition in 1969, fifteen percent
had judgment suspended, six percent involved discharge with warning, fifty-six
percent were placed on probation, eight percent were placed in a private facility,
ten percent in a state training school, and three percent entailed other placement.
Ibid., p. 91.

[170]See Calif. Civ. Code § 4506; Colo. Rev. Stat. § 46-1-6 (1972); and Ky. Rev.
Stat. Ann. §§ 403.140, 403.170 (1972).

proposed Uniform Marriage and Divorce Act,[171] fails to adequately protect the welfare of children and there is a real danger that the parties and the court will overlook their interests in a hurried disposition of divorce cases. The conspicuous lack of meaningful guidelines or definitions of *breakdown* and the failure to tie-in divorce-upon-demand with conciliation or counseling services tends to make divorce a virtually automatic administrative reflex rather than a reasoned judgment. There are no brakes on impetuous divorce where there is no screening as to the viability of the marriage. Live marriages may be interred along with dead ones, attention is focused upon the demand of one party, and the interests of the other party and the children may go by default.

Of course, even under traditional divorce law, the procedure tends to be *pro forma* where each wants a divorce so that usually the separation agreement of the parties is rubber stamped without any check on the special interests of children.[172] That danger is compounded, however, where only one party desires a divorce and may obtain it upon demand. It constitutes a gross neglect of the public interest in the welfare of children to permit divorce upon unilateral demand without protective devices to assure a careful check on whether or not there is adequate protection of their future. In Canada and England,[173] regardless of the breakdown of the marriage, a divorce may be denied if it would occasion hardship to the children. Although that extreme may be undesirable, at a minimum some court official should have responsibility for protecting the welfare of children upon parental divorce and the surest safeguard is independent representation by counsel to offset the dangers of automatic divorce.

---

[171]The Uniform Marriage and Divorce Act was drafted by the National Conference of Commissioners on Uniform State Laws in 1970 and amended in 1971, but as yet has not received approval of the American Bar Association. Section 310 of the Uniform Act gives a court discretion to appoint an attorney to represent a child with reference to custodial and support issues.

[172]Over ninety percent of American divorce cases are uncontested and frequently a separation agreement precedes the divorce and establishes the custodial and support terms of the decree. Unless objection is raised, such terms usually are accepted by the court.

[173]See Rev. Stat. Canada Ch. D-8 (1970), and Canada Divorce Act, 1967-68, C. 24 § 1, 4, 7, 8; and the English Divorce Reform Act (1969 C. 55).

CHAPTER SIX

TO EARN AND KEEP HIS OWN EARNINGS

and to be emancipated from the parent-child relationship when that relationship has broken down
and he has left home due to abuse, neglect, serious
family conflict, or other sufficient cause, and when
his best interests would be served by the termination of parental authority.

PERHAPS IT IS UNIMPORTANT, except to a child, that according to
common law doctrine he has no right to keep his own earnings. Under feudalistic principles, his father is entitled to his
services or side income in exchange for the father's duty of support.[174] Wives were under a similar onus at common law but the
Married Women's Property Acts[175] of the last century emancipated them from the system. Except for occasional statutes de-
signed to cover the child prodigy in sports or entertainment,[176]
the status of children as property owners or income producers remains much the same as it was in medieval times.

The common law rules are obsolete and contrary to prevailing mores. It may come as a surprise to many parents to learn
that legally they are entitled to their son's earnings from his news-
paper route or baby-sitting money saved by their daughter. It
would be natural to assume that the laborer is worthy of his hire.
Another anachronism is that what is given to the child by way of
support and maintenance and for purposes of education, such as
clothing, school books, etc., belongs to the parent who may reclaim
it or recover damages for its injury.[177] Moreover, property pur-
chased with the earnings of the child, which has not been given to
him, belongs to the parent.[178]

---

[174]See Madden: Persons and Domestic Relations (1931), p. 439.
[175]See Clark: Law of Domestic Relations (1968) p. 22ff.
[176]For example, see New York Gen. Oblig. Law § 105 et seq.
[177]Madden, note 174 at 440.
[178]*Ibid.*

The common law rule that minors are not entitled to their own earnings denigrates them and relegates them to an inferior status and at the same time is unfair. Since the rule may be abridged by agreement or subject to an estoppel,[179] its repeal may not be imperative, although abrogation would eliminate the insult.

The common law status of minority obviously required a suspension of some of the incidents of such status in appropriate situations. The concept of emancipation served in that regard with reference to the economic incident of the relationship. Under both Roman law and common law, emancipation is basically an economic doctrine or a recognition of economic independence and it is not synonomous with attainment of the age of majority.[180] Emancipation may occur at any chronological age and has the consequence of relieving the minor of parental control and the duty of rendering filial services and terminating the parent's duty of support, maintenance, and education. Other incidents of the status of minority, however, survive and emancipation does not mean that a minor achieves adulthood so as to become a legal person. For example, a seventeen-year-old minor who marries is still subject to statutory regulations based on an age of majority set at twenty-one or eighteen years of age.[181]

It is important to note that historically emancipation has been regarded as the unilateral privilege of the parent. It is not the prerogative of a minor to emancipate himself. Emancipation oc-

---

[179]See Fraser: Guardianship of the person, *Iowa L Rev, 45:*239, 1960.

[180]See Clark: *Law of Domestic Relations* (1968) p. 240f. It should be noted that some states, particularly in the South, permit a minor to petition for emancipation, and if the court is satisfied that the minor really is self-sufficient, an emancipation decree may issue.

[181]Miller v. United States, 123 F.2d 715 (C.C.A.8th, 1942). At common law majority was attained the day preceding the twenty-first anniversary of birth, on the first moment of that day. See Ex parte Wood, 5 Cal. App. 471, 90 P. 961 (1907). Of course, by statute, an earlier age than twenty-one may be set for attaining majority, but constitutional problems arise if a different age of majority is set for females and males. See Vlasak v. Vlasak, 204 Minn. 331, 283 N.W. 489 (1939). The fixing of the age of majority at twenty-one (except at eighteen for the sovereign) was purely arbitrary and probably related to the ability to bear arms and the completion of training in knighthood. See James: The age of majority, *Amer J Leg Hist, 4:*22, 1960.

curs with the express or implied consent of the parents but in some states may be effected by law where a parent has been guilty of such outrageous behavior that parental rights should be forfeited.[182]

Implied emancipation originally covered situations where a minor left home for good and set up an independent household and his parents acquiesced by doing nothing about it. A son by taking a job and moving out of the home, or perhaps by entering military service, became emancipated from the economic incidents of the parent-child relationship.[183] A daughter who married thereby emancipated herself although some cases hold that the marriage must have been with parental consent.[184] Of course, the concept of emancipation merely cuts off the parent's legal duty of support and does not affect any moral obligation that may exist nor preclude gifts to a son in military service or to a married daughter. Moreover, equitable considerations may preclude a finding of emancipation, and public welfare laws may impose a support obligation on parents even though a child has been emancipated or has reached majority.[185]

A tendency to disregard the unilateral character of emancipation so as to promote the interests of children may be seen in cases where there is emancipation by law without express or implied parental consent. A leading Maryland case held that children were emancipated and that their guardian could sue the father's estate where he had killed the mother in their presence and then committed suicide.[186] Thereby they obtained a money judgment in addition to their inheritance. Other cases have held that emancipation took place where a father injured his children due to

---

[182]See Manhke v. Moore, 197 Md. 61, 77 A.2d 923 (1951), and Cowgill v. Boock, 189 Or. 282, 218 P.2d 445 (1950).

[183]See 20 A.L.R.2d 1414 (1951), but compare Wack v. Wack, 74 N.Y.S.2d 573 (1st Dept. 1944), with Craig v. Craig, 24 A.D.2d 588, 262 N.Y.S.2d 398 (2d Dept. 1965).

[184]See Commonwealth v. Graham, 157 Mass. 73, 31 N.E. 706 (1892), and Austin v. Austin, 167 Md. 164 (1911), but compare Wolf v. Wolf, 194 App. Div. 33, 185 N.Y.S. 37 (1920), and see 58 A.L.R.2d 355 (1958).

[185]Clark: *Law of Domestic Relations* (1968), p. 241.

[186]Manke v. Moore, 197 Md. 61, 77 A.2d 923 (1951).

reckless driving,[187] the obvious purpose being to avoid the parental immunity doctrine so as to collect damages from an insurance company. The doctrine of estoppel also may be used in such situations in lieu of an expanded concept of emancipation.[188]

Permanent termination of parental rights by court order also emancipates a child from the control of his natural parents, although he becomes a ward of the court or someone who stands *in loco parentis* succeeds to parental rights and duties. Neglect petitions may be filed in most states where the home environment is dangerous to the health, safety, or morals of a child.[189] Usually, if neglect is established, the court may order either a temporary or permanent termination of parental rights. The statutes are couched in vague language as to what constitutes neglect. For example, in New York, neglect may be established by proof that there is inadequate care, maintenance and protection, lack of supervision or moral guidance, or abandonment of the child.[190] For a permanent termination of parental rights there must be overwhelming evidence to support such a drastic order, although a temporary termination may be sustained on a lesser quantum of proof.

A temporary termination of parental rights may involve a removal of the child from parental control so that a specific purpose may be achieved. Thus, the child of a Jehovah's Witness may be removed from parental control so that a guardian's consent may be given to a blood transfusion needed by the child.[191] Courts may be reluctant, however, to supersede parental control and an interesting New York decision refused to do so in order to direct an operation to correct a hair lip and a cleft palate.[192] Perhaps the fact that surgery rather than mere treatment was required offset the psychological testimony as to the detriment the

---

[187]For example, see Cowgill, v. Boock, 189 Or. 282, 218 P.2d 445 (1950).

[188]See Prosser: *Law of Torts* (4th ed., 1971), 866-67, for citation of cases holding that a reckless parent *forfeits* his parental immunity.

[189]See, for example, New York Fam. Ct. Act § 312.

[190]*Ibid.*

[191]Levitsky v. Levitsky, 231 Md. 388, 190 A.2d 621 (1963). See also Note: Judicial power to order medical treatment for minors over the objection of their guardians, *Syracuse L Rev, 14*:84, 1962.

[192]In Re Seiferth, 309 N.Y. 80, 127 N.E.2d 820 (1955).

condition would occasion. In any event, the subsequent career of the minor in question proved that the dire predictions of the expert witnesses were not justified in his particular case and that he could achieve success and a good social adjustment despite, or perhaps because of, his disfigurement.[193]

State intervention into the common law control of children by parents has been pervasive. Since the last century courts and legislatures have increasingly intruded into areas that formerly were autonomous and a matter of parental prerogative.[194] Although in this country there never has been the equivalent of a Roman *patria potestas,* parental powers formerly were substantial if not absolute. Today, parents are subject to judicial control and may not have the last say in the upbringing of children. They may not oust courts of jurisdiction by their private agreement as to custody, visitation, or child support.[195] The widespread interest in the family is manifested by the activities of many professions and authorities. What formerly was private domain has become the concern of governmental and social agencies, school, church, and other authorities. Such concern reflects both humanitarian impulses and a recognition that the traditional agencies of control have broken down in that parents no longer can effectively wield the authority that is theirs in theory. The school and the church also have diminished authority so governmental agencies and the law have moved to fill the void.

There is some precedent that a child may purchase necessaries not provided by parents and that the latter are liable therefor to suppliers,[196] or that a child may himself sue a parent for sup-

[193]See Goldstein and Katz: *The Family and the Law* (1965), p. 993.

[194]See Katz: *When Parents Fail* (1971), pp. 4-5.

[195]See Foster and Freed: *Law and the Family—New York* (1966), § 29:1. See also, Smith v. Smith, 7 Ohio App.2d 4, 218 N.E.2d 473 (1964), and Rouse v. State 184 So.2d 839 (Ala. Ct. App. 1966), involving child support. It also may be of interest that liability for alimony or child support is not discharged by bankruptcy proceedings. See 11 U.S.C. § 35; Dunbar v. Dunbar, 190 U.S. 340 (1903); Matter of LoGrasso, 23 F. Supp. 340 (W.D.N.Y. 1938); and Adams v. United States, 65 F. Supp. 86 (Ct. Claims 1946).

[196]See Girls Latin School of Chicago v. Hart, 317 Ill. App. 382, 46 N.E.2d 118 (1943), and Auringer v. Cochrane, 225 Mass. 273, 114 N.E.2d 355 (1916).

port.[197] Moreover, where a minor is an heir, a guardian is appointed to protect his interests, and guardianship of a child's property may arise in other situations.[198] It is assumed that there is inherent judicial power under the *parens patriae* doctrine to authorize intervention into the parent-child relationship and to subject parental authority to judicial review and legal safeguards.

The state also in its exercise of police power regulates various activities on the basis of age. Typically, there may be a statutory age of majority set at twenty-one or eighteen; a voting age of eighteen; an age set for capacity to marry, to buy or drink liquor, or to purchase cigarettes, etc. There is, in addition to this, the child labor laws.[199] As is true with regard to tests of mental competence for various activities, there is a general age of majority and differing ages for other functions. In a sense, legislative designation of specific ages for particular functions undermines the dichotomy between majority and minority and may permit the inference that legislative hunch rather than reason has been determinative. On the other hand, age differentiation also may be a recognition of the limits of effective regulation and control and the customs or mores of our youth culture.

Even though it be conceded that any age selected for attaining majority or for participation in various so-called adult activities is inevitably an arbitrary classification, it does not follow that all attempts at age differentials must be abandoned. Rather, what is needed is a periodic review of ages set and a re-examination in terms of function and efficacy. It is necessary and reasonable to set an age for driving licenses, for induction into military service, for the age of consent, and for the right to vote or to marry, but to be effective the age set must be realistic. The differentiation should

---

[197]See McQuade v. McQuade, 145 Colo. 218, 358 P.2d 470 (1960), and cases collected in Annot., 13 A.L.R.2d 1142 (1950).

[198]See Clark: *Law of Domestic Relations* (1968), p. 244f.

[199]The stipulation of different ages for different functions existed even in feudal times. II Pollock and Maitland: *History of English Law,* (2d ed., 1959), pp. 438-439, states that "there is more than one 'full age.' The young burgess is of full age when he can count money and measure cloth; the young sokeman when he is fifteen, the tenant by knight's service when he is twenty-one years old. . . . The military tenant is kept in ward until he is twenty-one years old; the tenant in socage is out of ward six or seven years earlier. . . ."

have a reasonable basis in terms of the general maturity and be-havior of youth with reference to the particular activity. The leg-islative judgment in this regard is entitled to considerable leeway as is shown by the Supreme Court's decisions on obscenity.[200]

Of immediate concern is a reconsideration of the concept of emancipation. Why should emancipation be a parental preroga-tive but not a privilege of minors? At some stage of child develop-ment a continued parent-child relationship should be a matter of mutual consent insofar as control and the economic incidents are concerned. Although not recognized officially, such already is a phenomenon of modern life. Thousands of nomadic minors flock to big cities and congregate in Greenwich Village, Haight-As-bury, Harvard Square, or the local equivalent. In legal theory they are unemancipated and subject to parental control; as mi-nors they may lack capacity to consent to medical care or treat-ment, or to counseling and guidance; and as runaways they may be arrested and returned to the home from which they fled.[201] Common law and traditional rules simply do not work effectively and are too cumbersome. The status of minority may inhibit or bar their care and protection and legal guardianship may be im-practical.

One device which might meet some of the needs of runaway youths is the office of a public guardian who would have the authority of a surrogate parent and who would be empowered to consent to welfare, medical and other services for minors who

---

[200]See Ginsberg v. New York, 390 U.S. 629 (1968) (conviction sustained for selling material "harmful to minors"), but compare Butler v. Michigan, 352 U.S. 380 (1957) (reversing conviction for offering for sale to public material deleterious to youths).

[201]Some states have adopted the Uniform Interstate Compact on Juveniles which is intended to facilitate the return of runaways to their families. In addi-tion, most states have provisions in their juvenile codes which apply to the run-away situation. For example, under New York Family Court Act § 718, provision is made for the return of runaways (males under sixteen or females under eigh-teen) and a child's refusal to give his name, or the name and address of his legal custodian, or whose statement is reasonably doubted, justify the officer's conclu-sion that he has run away without just cause. However, the officer instead of re-turning him to his legal custodian, may place him in a detention facility but not in the police station. See also, State v. Macri, 495 P.2d 355 (Utah 1972), which discusses duty regarding runaways.

have left home. The primary obligation of such a guardian would be to serve the best interests of the minor, and, where proper, to preserve confidentiality with reference to matters communicated to him. His responsibility would be to deal with the minor as a person, to provide constructive help, and to see that the minor received proper care and protection. To be effective, such a guardian would counsel and advise, and by persuasion rather than orders, would seek to reunite the family where that is feasible; where impossible, he would seek to provide such security as was available for the minor's life on his own. An emphasis would be placed on social services, not on legal rights and remedies. It would be necessary for the public guardian to have an office or branch office at the locations where runaways congregate.

Statutory authority will be necessary in order to create such a public guardian and in addition there must be a redefinition of *emancipation*. It is suggested that a minor should be entitled to emancipate himself where the parent-child relationship has broken down and the child has left home due to abuse, neglect, serious conflict or other sufficient cause which cannot be resolved, and where his best interests will be served by a termination of parental authority. Depending upon age, there may or may not be any need for the protection of a public or other guardian. There also may be a need to relax compulsory school attendance laws for emancipated children and to amend child labor laws so that they may be employed. Laws, rules, and regulations pertaining to the medical care of minors should be modified so that a minor may give an effective consent for medical treatment and counseling.

CHAPTER SEVEN

TO BE FREE OF LEGAL DISABILITIES

or incapacities save where such are convincingly shown to be necessary and protective of his actual best interests.

THE WOMEN'S LIBERATION MOVEMENT has raised and confirmed the suspicion that some legal disabilities for ulterior purposes have been imposed under the guise of protective measures.[202] The same may be true of some of the disabilities of minority. Paternalistic measures may be more protective of ancient paternal prerogatives than of the best interests of minors. Moreover, the need for a particular disability or incapacity may no longer exist and there may be no current justification for its perpetuation.

The most obvious instance of currently questionable regulation and restriction is to be found in compulsory school attendance and child labor laws. Typically, state law requires that children attend school for full time instruction between the ages of six and sixteen.[203] Unless schools provide a meaningful educational experience, it is impossible to justify compulsory attendance laws unless it is assumed that the police power includes preventive detention in order to keep children off the streets.[204] Although courts may be reluctant to face such an issue, it seems clear that many city schools are mere ware housing operations,

---

[202]See Kanowitz: *Women and the Law* (1968), p. 179.

[203]See for example, New York Educat. Law § 3205 et seq (McKinney's Ann. Stat. 1972).

[204]Compulsory school attendance laws have been sustained even against the claim that they abridged freedom of religion. See State v. Garber, 197 Kan. 567, 419 P.2d 896 (1966). However, In re Foster, 69 Misc. 2d 400, 330 N.Y.S.2d 8 (Fam. et. 1972), held that parents who refused to send their daughters to school in their district because they were afraid for their safety and enrolled them in another district, giving a false address, were not guilty of neglect when they kept their daughters home after they were discharged from the second school.

and some might fairly be described as maximum security institutions. In such an atmosphere the educational function becomes secondary or meaningless. Regardless of who is to blame, the fact remains that some children are coerced by law into participating in what at best may be a meaningless education if they are compelled to attend school. It no longer may be assumed that every school meets its educational commitment even though a majority may do so. The same principles which support the proposition that juvenile delinquents and mental patients have a right to treatment[205] apply here as well, since institutionalization is involuntary and is conditioned upon the provision of a meaningful program.

If the deterioration of some public schools continues, and school dropouts increase, compulsory attendance laws may become dead letters. The social consequences may be severe unless job training and employment opportunities are opened up for high school dropouts. Many teenagers might be better off in apprenticeship work or vocational training but are now the captives of compulsory school attendance laws and are frozen into an unproductive routine.

Unemployment is a disability of youth. The general pattern is that all wage employment is barred to children under fourteen, all employment during school hours is forbidden to those under sixteen, and hazardous jobs may not be filled by those under eighteen.[206] There may or may not be justification for a particular classification of *hazardous,* and it is noteworthy that sixteen-year-olds are deemed to be old enough to apply for learner's permits or to drive automobiles, and that seventeen year olds may enlist for military service. In some cases, the label of *hazardous*

---

[205]See Robitscher: Courts, state hospitals, and the right to treatment, *Amer J Psychiat, 129:*3, 1972; Rubin: Children as the victims of institutionalization, *Child Welfare, 60:*6, 1972; and report of the Committee on Mental Health Services Inside and Outside the Family Court in the City of New York, entitled "Juvenile Justice Confounded: Pretensions and realities in Treatment Services" (1972).

[206]See New York Educ. Law § 3215 (McKinney's Ann. Stat. 1972), which makes it unlawful to employ in any trade, business or services a minor under eighteen who does not have an employment permit, subject to some exceptions, viz. serving as a caddy, baby sitter, or doing yard work or domestic chores, if over fourteen years old.

may reflect a monopoly by adults of certain occupations. In addition, an artificial barrier is created in some instances by requiring a high school diploma in order to hold certain jobs. The state, generally effectively, regulates age requirements by the issuance of employment certificates, which are difficult for those under eighteen to acquire. To be a caddy in New York, a boy must be over fourteen, and the same age is set for girls who wish to serve as baby sitters.[207] Interestingly, no employment certificate is required for household chores or casual work, and state minimum wage laws usually authorize lower rates for minors, as do the laws pertaining to farm workers.[208] Such exceptions may permit exploitation and wage discrimination against minors.

The combination of compulsory school attendance and child labor laws is a major factor contributing to unrest and crime in many city areas. There may be no reasonable alternatives for a ghetto youth whose school is a custodial institution and where he is barred from access to meaningful work. Unless flexibility is achieved, the system is bound to fail.

There are many other disabilities and incapacities of youth, some of which have been previously mentioned. In addition to limitations on ownership of property, and the traditional family immunity doctrine, there is the area of commercial activity. The general rule is that infants have a privilege to disaffirm their contracts and lack full capacity to contract, and that such incapacity persists until age twenty-one unless the legislature has set a lower age.[209] However, the impracticality of the rule is attested by the numerous exceptions. For example, an infant may be bound by his contract for *necessaries*.[210] Moreover, if an infant exercises

---

[207]*Ibid.*

[208]*Ibid.*

[209]The minor may make a contract and enforce it but he has a privilege of disaffirmance. See Holt v. Clarencieux, 2 Str. 957 (1732); 2 Williston, Contracts, ch. 9 (3d ed. 1959). If he chooses not to disaffirm, the contract may be enforced against an adult.

[210]See Gregory v. Lee, 64 Conn. 407, 30 A. 53 (1894); Annot. 71 A.L.R. 226 (1931); and 2 Williston, Contracts § 241 (3d ed. 1959). The infant also may make a binding contract to borrow money to use for necessaries. See Annot., 65 A.L.R. 1337 (1930).

his privilege to disaffirm a contract, he may be required to make a good faith effort to return the goods.[211]

The infant's privilege of disaffirmance must be exercised within a reasonable time before or after he reaches majority.[212] If he is a child prodigy or athlete, special statutes may apply.[213] Depending on his age, a minor may contract a valid marriage even though statutes provide for parental consent until he reaches majority.[214] The public policy basis for the usual incapacity of an infant to contract and his privilege of disaffirmance is said to be his lack of mature judgment and his vulnerability to overreaching.

Although there has been substantial modification of the notion that a minor should not be bound by his contracts, as by lowering the age at which he is bound, or by exempting certain transactions, the usual attacks on the rule have been in terms of the hardship which may be occasioned to sellers when an infant disaffirms his contract.[215] The usual rule also does harm to the minor. Behavioral science assures us with confidence that responsibility is not promoted by making people irresponsible.[216] The

---

[211]Clark: Law of Domestic Relations (1968), 238. "Most of the cases hold that if the child still has the consideration, he must return it upon disaffirmance, but if he has lost or dissipated it, he may disaffirm without being required to give it back. . . . In a few jurisdictions the child must restore the consideration in all cases where the other party was not guilty of fraud or bad faith, and where the contract was reasonably fair and prudent."

[212]Wuller v. Chuse Grocery Co., 241 Ill. 398, 89 N.E. 796 (1909); Clark, note 211 at 236.

[213]California and New York are among the states having such statutes. See Cal. Civ. Code § 36, and New York Gen. Oblig. Law § 3-105. See also, Note, U. Chic. L. Rev. 16:183, 1948.

[214]Under the annulment laws of most states, lack of parental consent does not effect the validity of a marriage and is not a ground for annulment, and parents have no standing to seek an annulment. See Castor v. United States, 174 F.2d 481 (C.A.8 1949), cert. denied, 338 U.S. 836 (1949), and Clark, Law of Domestic Relations 79 (1968).

[215]Clark: Law of Domestic Relations (1968), p. 239.

[216]For example see Baldwin: Theories of Child Development (1968) where there is a discussion and comparison of various theories of child development including the S-R (stimulus-response) theory. Roche: The Criminal Mind (paperback ed. 1958) p. 243 says the following with reference to the treatment of criminals: "If we regard a prison as a kind of kindergarden for grownups who failed to grow up, operated on authoritarian principle, we can appreciate that rehabilitation under such tutelage does not equip its graduates for democratic adaptation; rather we would expect that such rehabilitation has a large influence in shaping the antisocial potential. Here we have child-rearing at its worst."

minor who is permitted to welch on his commitments may find sellers who refuse to sell, so that his supposed protection boomerangs. In theory he may own the money in his pocket but he is limited as to what he can do with it. In real life, however, transactions are carried on by minors, and ordinarily the question of infancy is not raised.

It would be in the interest of minors and adults to adopt a general rule that infants have full capacity to contract and are bound by their agreements, but that those dealing with them are subject to familiar rules as to fraud, duress, and mistake, which take into account the immaturity of the minor, the experience of the other party, and the nature of the bargain. Such a rule of contracts law would be analagous to the tort rule that an infant is liable for his torts but that his negligence may be judged in terms of a *reasonable infant* as distinguished from a reasonable man.[217]

The parent-child immunity doctrine still persists in some states despite the proliforation of exceptions and the trend for its repudiation.[218] The two major factors which led to the abandonment of the doctrine are the belated conviction that the immunity was not in the best interests of the family and the assumed presence of insurance.[219] Those states which still adhere to the doctrine claim that the immunity preserves domestic tranquility and prevents fraud on an insurer.[220] Both the doctrine and its rationale are no longer convincing and most states which have reconsidered the matter have abolished the immunity thus permitting minors to exercise a most important personal right, even though it must be done through a guardian *ad litem* or next friend.[221]

There are many other examples of disabilities and incapacities. In most states a minor may not hold a public or administrative office; he cannot be admitted to many professions; he cannot

---

[217]See Prosser, On Torts, § 128 (3d ed. 1964), and Gremban v. Burke, 33 Wis.2d 1, 146 N.W.2d 453 (1966).

[218]See McCurdy, Torts Between Parent and Child, 5 Vill L. Rev. 521 (1960).

[219]See Gelbman v. Gelbman 25 N.Y.2d 434 297 N.Y.S.2d 529 245 N.E.2d 192 (1969). The case which established the immunity was Hewelette v. George, 68 Miss. 703, 9 So. 885 (1891), involving an alleged false imprisonment in a mental hospital.

[220]See Clark: *Law of Domestic Relations* (1968) p. 257f.

[221]*Ibid.*

make a will; he cannot consent to certain relationships; he lacks capacity to acquire his own domicile of choice; he cannot serve on a jury; and generally he cannot consent to medical care and treatment.[222] Although frequently subject to exceptions, such disabilities usually apply until adulthood is achieved and without regard to the fact that a particular minor or minors in general have sufficient maturity of judgment and experience to be granted autonomy for the particular purpose or function.

It should be clear from the above brief discussion of disabilities and incapacities that such incidents of status have been eroded by time and changing conditions. It is not enough, however, to chisel away at hardship instances, and there is a current need to change the philosophical base so that children will be recognized as legal persons, and hence removed from their common law status as non-persons. There must be strong justification for any impairment for their legal rights and for the imposition of any disabilities or incapacities. It is naive to assume that rules derived from feudal times are actually protective and serve the best interests of modern children.

---

[222]*Ibid.,* § 8.1.

CHAPTER EIGHT

TO SEEK AND OBTAIN MEDICAL CARE AND TREATMENT AND COUNSELING

THE GENERAL DISABILITIES and incapacities of minority discussed in Chapter Seven receive their most questionable application where a minor needs medical care and treatment or counseling and the importance of the problem warrants the expression of the stated principle and separate discussion. In the health area, the disability of minority may literally be a life and death matter as well as a restriction on human freedom.

One would suppose that a genuine concern for the welfare of children would be expressed most positively where their physical or mental health was at stake. Of course they should have the legal right to receive, as needed, medical care and treatment and should have the further right to seek and obtain professional counseling. But here again autonomy is denied and the consequence of status is that minors lack capacity to give a valid consent. Such is the broad common law or general rule, but fortunately there are significant exceptions and recently several state legislatures have enacted general or specific statutes in order to eliminate the problem.

Unquestionably, the requirement of parental consent for medical treatment deters large numbers of minors from seeking and obtaining medical attention when needed or as early as is desirable. Moreover, the medical profession is aware of the rule and in order to avoid litigation doctors often refuse to accept minors as patients without parental consent. Statutory elimination or modification of the common law rule is necessary so that minors may seek and doctors will be willing to give necessary health services to minors. This does not mean, however, that doctors should not consult with parents and proceed on the basis of their consent in the normal situation where the parent is expected to pay the medical bill and there is no violation of the child's confidence. Authority to suspend the usual requirement of parental consent is needed for exceptional situations, as for example, where the family no longer is intact or where there is a problem which the minor is unwilling or emotionally unable to communicate to his family.

Pregnancy, contraceptive information, drug abuse, venereal disease, and emotional disturbances are among the sensitive problems where a rule requiring parental consent to health services may be counterproductive. Unfortunately, it cannot be assumed that such sensitive problems are rare or virtually non-existent. Appalling statistics show the contrary. Moreover, minors with such problems are not now getting the medical care they need. The teenage unmarried mother is about three times as likely to have a premature baby as a married mother, fetal deaths are twice as high, and maternal deaths are four times as great.[223] Good early pre-natal care could eliminate the above disparities. To insist upon parental consent may imperil the life of the mother or the child.

Although it is true, as previously stated, that courts have power to suspend or terminate parental control and rights in order to permit medical care and treatment for children, such procedure may be protracted and cumbersome. The assumption of a guardianship for medical purposes is and should be an ultimate remedy but it is unsatisfactory for many of the sensitive problems confronting children. Litigation or the involvement of strangers may not be practicable.

The minor's claim to autonomy may be most controversial when we consider the minor's interest in contraceptive information and services or in abortion. Looked at realistically, it is obvious that sexually active adolescents and teenagers need and should have access to counseling and contraceptive services upon demand because usually they already have rejected parental control and advice. The practical consequence of withholding counseling and services unless parental consent is obtained is likely to

---

[223]Wiss: Position Paper on Medical Care and the Minor (1971), an unpublished paper prepared for the Conference on the Rights of Minors, held at New York University in October 1971.

be more disasterous for all concerned than a fancied usurpation of parental authority.[224] It also is realistic to concede that the sex problems of teenagers is a sensitive area for parents as well as minors and that legislatures and courts also may shy away from the problem. It is nonetheless clear that the interests of society as well as those of minors should take precedence over parental authority in regard to counseling and contraceptive services. The staggering cost of aid to teenage unwed mothers and other welfare programs involving unwed mothers and their children removes the problem from the private domain.[225]

The legal right of a teenage girl to procure an abortion without parental consent is a more complicated matter and the law in that regard is far from clear. Although the Supreme Court has held that in early pregnancy an abortion is a matter for the private decision of physician and patient and that the patient's consent removes the procedure from the ambit of criminal law,[226] the problem of capacity to consent remains. Under the New York statute, a female's consent to an abortion is legally effective but no age is specified.[227] Hospitals in New York City have been advised that parental consent may be dispensed with if the girl is seventeen or more years old.[228] California, on the other hand, has held that under their law parental consent is unnecessary and that a teenage girl may give an effective consent to an abortion.[229]

It may be argued that the decision to have an abortion is precisely the kind of decision a distraught young girl should not make on her own, not only because of immaturity of judgment, but also because of the emotional dimension of the decision. It may be

---

[224]*Ibid.*

[225]Currently the A.F.D.C. program is costing more than two billion dollars per year, and a substantial portion of that sum goes to unwed mothers and their children.

[226]Jane Roe *et al.* v. Wade, 93 S. Ct. 705 (1973), and Mary Roe v. Bolton, 93 S. Ct. 739 (1973).

[227]New York Laws 1970, Ch. 127, Revised Penal Law § 125.05, provides that "An abortional act is justified when committed upon a female with her consent by a duly licensed physician acting (a) under a reasonable belief that such is necessary to preserve her life, or (b) within 24 weeks from the commencement of her pregnancy. . . ."

[228]Law Department, City of New York, Opinion No. 103, 310, June 25, 1970, p. 4.

[229]Ballard v. Anderson, 95 Cal. Rptr. 1, 484 P.2d 1345 (1971).

said that she lacks the ability to give an informed consent. On the other hand, from the standpoint of the pregnant girl, involvement of her parents may be the thing she most dreads, or the pregnancy itself may be part of her rebellion against parental authority.[230] To the extent that the new law of abortion reflects a policy of providing an alternative to criminal abortions, is viewed as a matter of privacy and as an appropriate matter for medical decision, it may be practicable to urge the involvement of parents where feasible. Where the pregnant girl has left home, or communication with the parents would violate her confidence or be harmful to her, to dispense with the need for parental consent might be more advantageous. Admittedly, the particular age of the pregnant girl and the total circumstances should affect the medical decision as to the need for parental consent. Perhaps it would be best to conclude that parental consent to an abortion is unnecessary, that it is a matter for the decision of physician and patient, but that it is prudent to involve the girl's parents when that involvement would be helpful to the minor. The administrative decision in New York that parental consent will be required if the unwed mother is under seventeen may not be realistic and is not justifiable as an inflexible rule.

Treatment of minors for venereal disease is far less controversial than counseling them as to contraceptive techniques or aborting them without parental consent. The legitimate public health concern dictates that treatment be given with or without parental consent. Any requirement for parental consent to the treatment of minors for venereal disease is medically and psychologically absurd and forty or more states have enacted statutes to permit minors to give a valid consent to examinations and treatment for venereal disease.[231] Such statutes have been enacted recently and have run into little opposition.

Counseling and psychiatric care and treatment is another area where the need for parental consent should be suspended when necessary for the welfare or protection of the minor. Since the

---

[230]See Herzog: Who are the unmarried mothers? *Children,* 9:157, 1962; Young: *Out of Wedlock.* 1954, pp. 16-80; and Vincent: *Unmarried Mothers.* 1961, pp. 55-119.
[231]Wiss, note 223.

emotional and mental problems of minors are often associated with intra-family conflicts, it may be necessary to counsel or treat the minor without parental involvement. It should be left to the professional to determine at what stage, if any, the parents should be brought into the picture. The minor's need for confidentiality may be intense, especially when the immediate problem involves sexual activity or drug abuse. Again, the combination of the interests of the minor and public health considerations outweigh the parental need to know. Moreover, the long term parental interest may coincide with the preservation of confidentiality.

We have been discussing situations where it would be contrary to the best interests of minor and society to always require parental consent to medical care and treatment. Admittedly, these are exceptional circumstances and ordinarily family involvement is desirable and in accord with the best interests of all concerned. Legislatures have found it necessary to create exceptions to the general rule that minors lack capacity to consent to medical care and treatment. In addition, there are judge made exceptions.

The most important exception is that parental consent is unnecessary in emergency situations where there is imminent danger to the life or health of the minor and where parental consent cannot be readily obtained.[232] In some states this exception is codified,[233] while in others a person who stands *in loco parentis* may be given authority to consent to the medical procedure.[234] The exception is quite broad and, insofar as most operative procedures are concerned, will protect the doctor and the hospital from an assault and battery type action unless the failure to consult with the parents was inexcusable.

The general rule of the common law also does not apply to emancipated minors who are held to have capacity to consent to medical procedures and counseling.[235] This exception has been

[232]See Prosser: *Law of Torts*. 4th ed. 1971, 103; and Sullivan v. Montgomery, 155 Misc. 448, 279 N.Y.S. 2d 575 (1935).

[233]For example, see Mass. Gen. Laws Ann. Ch. 112, § 12D (1970); Md. Ann. Code art. 43 § 135 (1971); Miss. Code Ann. § 7129-81 (1966); and Pa. Stat. tit. 35, § 10104 (1969).

[234]*Ibid.*

[235]The leading case on consent to medical treatment and exceptions to the general rule is Bonner v. Moran, 126 F.2d 121 (D.C. Cir. 1941).

expanded to accomodate the *mature minor* doctrine in some states under which a minor is held to have capacity to consent to medical procedure which is for his benefit if he understands the nature and consequences of the proposed course of treatment.[236] The difficulty with this exception is that there is no sure way of knowing in advance when a minor will be regarded as sufficiently mature to qualify for the exception, and in any event there remains the problem of whether or not there was an "informed consent" under the circumstances of the particular case.

There are numerous other statutory modifications of the general rule that a minor lacks capacity to consent to medical care and treatment. A few states, both before and after the change in voting age, have lowered the age for effective consent to medical treatment. In Oregon, any person fifteen or over may give such consent;[237] in Washington eighteen is the age of consent for all purposes;[238] and in Maryland, North Carolina, and Pennsylvania,[239] any person eighteen or over (and in Hawaii, nineteen or over)[240] may consent to medical treatment. Those states which recently have lowered the age of majority to eighteen presumably have empowered persons over that age to consent to medical treatment.

As previously stated, about forty states now permit minors to be treated for venereal disease without parental consent. At least fourteen states by statute provide that minors may consent to treatment relating to pregnancy,[241] and six states have statutes authorizing physicians to provide birth control information and services to minors without parental consent.[242] Still other statutes

---

[236]See Bach v. Long Island Jewish Hospital, 49 Misc.2d 207, 267, N.Y.S.2d 289 (Sup. Ct. 1966); Gulf & S.R. Co. v. Sulivan, 155 Miss. 448, 119 So. 501 (1929); and Lacey v. Laird, 166 Ohio St. 12, 139 N.E.2d 25 (1956) ("nose job").

[237]Wiss, note 223.

[238]*Ibid.* Kentucky, Michigan, North Dakota, Tennessee, and Vermont, and a number of other states make eighten the age of majority.

[239]*Ibid.*

[240]*Ibid.*

[241]*Ibid.* These states are Alaska, California, Delaware, Hawaii, Kansas, Maryland, Minnesota, Mississippi, Missouri, Montana, New Jersey, New Mexico, Pennsylvania and Virginia.

[242]*Ibid.* The states are Colorado, Illinois, Maryland, Oregon, Tennessee and Virginia.

authorizing such services have no restrictions as to age.[243] There also are specific statutes permitting minors to consent to treatment for drug addiction and still others permitting them to make blood donations.[244]

Perhaps the most comprehensive recent statute is that of Pennsylvania which allows medical treatment to be given to minors of any age, without parental consent, if an attempt to obtain consent would cause delay which would increase the risk to the minor's health or life or if it is an examination for a venereal disease.[245] The Pennsylvania statute also codifies the exceptions to the common law rule and specifically permits a minor over eighteen, who has graduated from high school, or who has become pregnant, to receive medical services without parental consent. The statute also provides that physicians may not be held liable for unauthorized treatment if in good faith they treat minors who profess that they do not need their parent's consent. The Pennsylvania approach is sound but it may be doubted that the age of eighteen is low enough.

A different approach has been taken in California[246] and Minnesota[247] where minors have capacity to consent to medical treatment if they live away from home and are managing their own affairs. This constitutes a statutory recognition of the emancipation exception. However, Minnesota also specifically permits the treatment of minors for alcohol, drug abuse, venereal disease, pregnancy, contraception not amounting to sterilization, and emotional or mental disorders.[248] Immunity from civil suit is accorded to doctors who honor such consent of minors.

The above examples of judicial and legislative modification of the general rule requiring parental consent for the medical treatment or counseling of minors show that the general rule has outlived its usefulness. Reinforced by the public concern as to child

---

[243]*Ibid.*

[244]*Ibid.* For example, see Ind. Stat. Ann. § 35-4412 (1969): Mass. Gen. Laws Ann. ch. 112, § 12D (1970); Mich. Comp. Laws Ann. ch. 335, § 335.221 (1970).

[245]See Pa. Stat. tit. 35, § 10104 (1969).

[246]Cal. Civ. Code § 25.6 (1967 Supp.).

[247]See Minn. S.F. No. No. 1496, Ch. 544, § 144, 344 (1971).

[248]*Ibid.*

health, the individual interest of children in having an independent right to seek health services is being increasingly recognized. Such interests are deemed to outweigh the traditional prerogatives of parental control. However, in the ordinary situation the lack of capacity to consent to medical procedures does no harm to the minor and the parents should be involved in any medical decision. It is the exceptional situation of actual or potential conflict of interests between parent and child, where the need for parental consent should be dispensed with. Existing legal procedures for guardianship or the temporary suspension of parental authority are impracticable and there is a need for statutory authority so that in advance the need for parental consent may be eliminated where the procedure is for the benefit of the minor and it would be unreasonable to withhold consent. Rather than stipulating an arbitrary age of consent, as in Pennsylvania, a more flexible standard is to be preferred, and in addition to repeating the usual exceptions to the common law rule, a sound statute should cover situations where the minor has left home or for satisfactory reasons refuses to bring his parents into the situation.

CHAPTER NINE

TO RECEIVE SPECIAL CARE, CONSIDERATION, AND PROTECTION

in the administration of law and justice so that his
best interests always are a paramount factor.

THUS FAR IN OUR DISCUSSION we have been concerned with re-moving some of the incidents of the common law status of minority. There also is a positive obligation to act affirmatively to better the lot of minors. Such is especially evident when minors are institutionalized, placed outside their homes, or are compelled to go to school. The exercise of such authority carries with it the duty to see that the child's welfare really is being served. There is no basis for an assumption that compulsory school attendance invariably is for the child's good or that an industrial school will rehabilitate or build character. If minors are to be captives, at home, school, or before a juvenile court, they are entitled to special care, consideration and protection.

It is difficult if not impossible to legislate proper etiquette for the parent-child relationship at home. A court cannot effectively order a parent to give love and affection to his child. At most, parental misfeasance is of judicial concern, except perhaps when a court is weighing custody and visitation rights. Schools, however, are a different matter. As public institutions they are subject to legislative and judicial control.

Until relatively recently there was little if any judicial check on the treatment of children by school authorities. School discipline generally was limited only by the self-restraint of those in authority.[249] Attendance at school was regarded as a child's

[249]Formerly, school attendance, although compulsory, was viewed as a privilege which might be conditioned upon whatever rules and regulation school authorities cared to promulgate. See Steier v. New York State Education Commissioner, 271 F.2d 13 (C.C.A. 2, 1959). The leading case establishing constitutional rights

privilege, but he had few if any rights. That situation has changed. The starting point for analysis is that children have a legal right to a meaningful education and since they are a captive audience, school authorities have a correlative duty to provide the same. No longer is school attendance a privilege the enjoyment of which is conditioned upon unquestioning compliance with whatever regulations those in authority impose.

Only recently has there been a belated recognition that students have standing to participate in making decisions which affect their lives at school. Now there is legal authority holding that arbitrary or unreasonable school regulations are a nullity, and that students have at least some constitutional rights.[250] School authorities violate the law if they disregard the rudiments of due process and fair procedure in handling students and in disciplinary proceedings. In particular, if the sanction may be suspension or expulsion from school, the basic requirements of due process of law are applicable.[251]

For example, in New York, before a student may be suspended for behavioral or medical reasons, he must be accorded a fair hearing by the principal, and the principal's decision is subject to appeal.[252] The student has a right to counsel of his choice at any hearing where suspension or expulsion may be ordered. Students and their parents have a right to know in advance the school's rules and parents have a right to group statistical records concerning the school, and to inspect their child's full school record at any time. A principal no longer may refuse a diploma if the child has completed his course of study. Subject only to reason-

---

for students is Dixon v. Alabama State Board of Education, 294 F.2d 150 (C.C.A. 5, 1961), and the most significant Supreme Court decision to date is Tinker v. DesMoines School District, 393 U.S. 503 (1969).

[250]*Ibid.* See also Wright: The constitution on the campus, *Vand L. Rev, 22:* 1027, 1969.

[251]See Seavey: Dismissal of students: "Due Process," *Harv L Rev, 70:*1406, 1957, for an early article on the subject. See also Madera v. Board of Education of the City of New York, 386 F.2d 778 (C.C.A.2, 1967); and Breen v. Kahl, 296 F. Supp. 702 (W.D. Wis, 1969).

[252]See New York Civil Liberties Union Student Rights Handbook for New York City.

able regulations, students have the rights of free speech, freedom of the press, and freedom of assembly. Again, subject only to reasonable limitations, students have the right to determine their own appearance as to dress or hair, to form political and social organizations, and to use school facilities. A pregnant student has a right to remain in school as long as physically possible. Finally, there are vague limitations on attempted invasions of student privacy or property by police or school authorities.

Although some states may not have an administrative declaration of student rights such as those enumerated above, there is a growing list of court decisions which confirm the general proposition that rules and regulations must be fair and reasonable and it is clear that students do have legal rights and may not be dealt with arbitrarily.[253] The status of being a student no longer is a servile one in so far as the law is concerned. It is to be hoped that school administrators will extend more than a begrudging acceptance to the newly won rights of students.

The proposition is emerging that students must be dealt with fairly as to all school activities and that school authorities must have sound reasons for restrictions. Most significantly, students will demand and receive the right to participate in decision making as it affects their lives at school. In New York, the Board of Education has recognized the right of students to "be involved in the process of developing curriculum and of establishing disciplinary policies."[254]

As has been pointed out in another connection, the most practical and effective way to make sure that children receive special care, consideration, and protection at school or before any adult authority is to provide for the implementation of the right to counsel. In a sense, the so-called "establishment" itself is an adversary system, as much so as our judicial process. Youth advocacy programs are being developed by and for students in order to train spokesmen for youth's point of view. Adults will have to listen and eventually may be compelled to re-examine many old assumptions of doubtful current validity. It is to be hoped that

---

[253]See Wright, note 250.
[254]See note 252.

CHAPTER TEN

CONCLUSION

W E HAVE TRIED TO GIVE, as Karl Llewellyn used to say, "the bare bones" for a bill of rights for children. Doubtlessly, many important interests and rights have been overlooked. Moreover, the emphasis has been upon the rights rather than the duties of minors. That has been so because children's rights have been sadly neglected, not because children have no duties or responsibilities. It also is clear that unless children are treated fairly and their rights are respected, it is idle to speak down to them about duty and responsibility.

As noted at the outset, of course the several principles here advanced may apply with varying force depending upon the age of the child and the particular circumstances. The general proposition should be, perhaps, that children should be granted individual freedom and autonomy commensurate with their maturation and development and the burden should be upon those who abridge such freedom to show that it is necessary and actually in the child's best interests.

With the handicap of poor memories adults often look back to their childhood as happy carefree days when there were no problems. The problems of children may differ from those of adults but they are still problems. We also tend to forget that children usually have a highly developed sense of fairplay and honor and are sensitive to injustice and bullying. Their relative helplessness may intensify what to us are minor wrongs or mere errors of adult judgment. To the child, to be treated unfairly is a double wrong, for in addition to any other error, there is an abuse of authority.

We profess a dedication to the best interests of children but do we serve them well? Do we really listen to them? It is time for adults to reckon with the child's point of view and for the law to treat minors as persons.[255] In return, adults and the law may receive respect, which is the condition for human understanding, out of which may come the implementation of principles such as those referred to in this discussion.

---

[255]The author has deliberately omitted any discussion or analysis of the legal rights, if any, of an embryo or fetus in the light of the Supreme Court decisions in Jane Roe *et al.* v. Wade, and Mary Doe v. Bolton, 93 S. Ct. 705, 739 (1973). There is no implication that the subject is unimportant nor that some of the opinions here expressed may not be relevant to the legal status of an unborn child.

CASES CITED

Adams v. United States, 65 F.Supp. 86 (Ct.Claims 1946)
Application of Gault, 99 Ariz. 181, 407 P.2d 760 (1965)
Application of Mittenthal, 37 Misc.2d 502, 235 N.Y.S.2d 729 (1962)
Auringer v. Cochrane, 225 Mass. 273, 114 N.E. 355 (1916)
Austin v. Austin, 167 Md. 164 (1911)

"Baby Lenore" case *(see* People *ex rel.* Scarpetta, etc., and Scarpetta
v. DiMartino, infra)
Bach v. Long Island Jewish Hospital, 49 Misc.2d 207, 267 N.Y.S. 2d
289 (1966)
Bachman v. Mejias, 1 N.Y. 2d 575, 136 N.E. 2d 866 (1956)
Ballard v. Anderson, 39 Cal. Rptr. 1, 484 P.2d 1345 (1971)
Barth v. Barth, 12 Ohio Misc. 141, 225 N.E.2d 866 (1967)
Bazeley v. Forder, [1868] L.R. 3 Q.E. 554
Berlin v. Berlin, 239 Md. 52, 210 A.2d 380 (1965)
Berlin v. Berlin, 21 N.Y. 2d 371, 235 N.E. 2d 109, cert. den'd, 393 U.S.
840 (1967)
Bonner v. Moran, 126 F.2d 121 (D.C. Cir. 1941)
Bradwell v. State, 16 Wall. (U.S.) 130 (1872)
Brashear v. Brashear, 71 Idaho 158, 228 P.2d 243 (1951)
Breen v. Kahl, 296 F. Supp. 702 (W.D. Wis. 1969)
Bronner v. Bronner, 278 S.W. 2d 530 (Tex.Civ.App. 1954)
Bush v. Bush, 163 So. 2d 858 (La. 1964)
Butler v. Michigan, 352 U.S. 380 (1957)

Castor v. United States, 174 F.2d 481 (C.A. 8 1949)
Chapsky v. Wood, 27 Kan. 650, 40 Am. Rep. 321 (1881)
Commonwealth v. Graham, 157 Mass. 73, 31N.E. 706 (1892)
Connecticut General Life Ins. Co. v. Johnson, 303 U.S. 77 (1938)
Cowgill v. Boock, 189 Ore. 282, 218 P. 2d 445 (1950)
Craig v. Craig, 24 A.D. 2d 588, 262 N.Y.S. 2d 398 (2d Dept. 1965)

Dixon v. Alabama State Bd. of Ed., 294 F. 2d 150 (C.A. 5 1961)
Dunbar v. Dunbar, 190 U.S. 340 (1903)
Dunn v. Dunn, 217 S.W. 2d 124 (Tex.Civ.App. 1949)

Ex parte Day, 189 Wash. 368, 65 P.2d 1049 (1937)
Ex parte Wood, 5 Cal. App. 471, 90 P. 961 (1907)

Finlay v. Finlay, 240 N.Y. 429, 148 N.E. 624 (1925)
Flanagan v. Flanagan, 247 P.2d 212 (Ore. 1952)
Ford v. Ford, 371 U.S. 187 (1962)
Freeland v. Freeland, 92 Wash. 482, 159 P. 698 (1916)

Gardner v. Pettit, 192 So. 2d 696 (Miss. 1967)
Gelbman v. Gelbman, 25 N.Y. 2d 434, 245 N.E. 2d 192 (1969)
Ginsberg v. New York, 390 U.S. 629 (1968)
Girls Latin School of Chicago v. Hart, 317 Ill.App. 382, 46 N.E. 2d 118
    (1943)
Glona v. American Guarantee Co., 391 U.S. 73 (1968)
Gomez v. Perez, 93 S.Ct. 872 (1973)
Greenspan v. Slate, 97 A.2d 390 (N.J. 1953)
Gregory v. Lee, 64 Conn. 407, 30 A. 53 (1894)
Gremban v. Burke, 33 Wis. 2d 1, 146 N.W. 2d 453 (1966)
Gulf & S.R. Co. v. Sullivan, 155 Miss. 448, 119 So. 501 (1929)

Hewelette v. George, 68 Miss. 703, 9 So. 885 (1891)
Hiecke v. Hiecke, 163 Wis. 555, 157 N.W. 747 (1916)
Holt v. Clarencieux, 2 Str. 957 (1732)
Husten v. Husten, 122 N.W. 2d 892 (Iowa 1963)

In re Application of Carlson, 181 Neb. 877, 152 N.W. 2d 98 (1967)
In re Adoption of a Child by P and Wife, 114 N.J.Super. 584, 277 A.2d
    566 (1971)
In re Foster, 69 Misc. 2d 400, 330 N.Y.S. 2d 8 (1972)
In re Gault, 407 P.2d 760 (1965)
In re Holmes, 379 Pa. 599, 109 A. 2d 523 (1954)
In re Lindwall's Will, 287 N.Y. 347, 39 N.E. 2d 907 (1942)
In re Revocation of Appointment of a Guardian, 271 N.E. 2d 621
    (Mass. 1971)
In re Rinker, 117 A.2d 780 (Pa. Super. 1955)
In re Seiferth, 309 N.Y. 480, 127 N.E. 2d 820 (1955)

Jenkins v. Jenkins, 173 Wis. 592, 181 N.W. 826 (1921)
Johnson v. Johnson, 7 Utah 2d 263, 323 P.2d 16 (1958)
Jones v. Koulos, 142 Colo. 92, 349 P.2d 704 (1960)

King v. DeManneville, 5 East 221, 102 Eng. Rep. 1054 (K.B. 1804)
Kovacs v. Brewer, 356 U.S. 604 (1958)
Kent v. United States, 383 U.S. 541 (1966)

Labine v. Vincent, 401 U.S. 532 (1971)
Lacey v. Laird, 166 Ohio St. 12, 139 N.E. 2d 25 (1956)
Lamar v. Harris, 117 Ga. 993, 44 S.E. 866 (1903)
Lamb v. State, 475 P.2d 829 (Okla. Crim. App. 1970)
Law Dept. N.Y.C. Op. No. 103
Lesser v. Lesser, (Discussed in Goldstein and Katz, The Family and
   the Law (1965)
Levitsky v. Levitsky, 231 Md. 388, 190 A.2d 621 (1963)
Levy v. Louisiana, 391 U.S. 68 (1968)

Madera v. Board of Education of N.Y.C., 386 F. 2d 778 (C.C.2 1967)
Mahnke v. Moore, 197 Md. 61, 77 A.2d 923 (1951)
Mason v. Zolnosky, 103 N.W.2d 752 (Iowa 1960)
Matter of Lo Grasso, 23 F.Supp. 340 (W.D.N.Y. 1938)
Matter of Vanderbilt, 245 App. Div. 211, 281 N.Y.S. 171 (1935)
Miller v. United States, 123 F.2d 715 (C.A.8 1942)
Montimore v. Wright, 6 Mees. & W. 482 (1842)
Muller v. Oregon, 208 U.S. 412 (1908)
McKiever v. Pennsylvania, 403 U.S. 528 (1971)
McGuire v. McGuire, 157 Neb. 226, 59 N.W. 2d 336 (1953)
McQuade v. McQuade, 145 Colo. 218, 358 P.2d 470 (1960)

Oregon v. Mitchell, 400 U.S. 112 (1970)

Painter v. Banister, 258 Iowa 1390, 140 N.W. 2d. 152 (1966)
Penn v. Abell, 173 S.W. 2d 483 (Tex.Civ.App. 1943)
Perry v. Simione, 107 Colo. 132, 239 P. 1056 (1925)
People v. Glendening, 259 App.Div. 384, 19 N.Y.S. 2d 693 (1940)
People *ex rel.* Halvey v. Halvey, 295 N.Y. 836, 66 N.E. 2d 861 (1946),
   aff'd 330 U.S. 610 (1947)
People *ex rel.* Scarpetta v. Spence-Chapin Adoption Agency, 28 N.Y.
   2d 185, 269 N.E. 2d 787 (1971) cert. den. 404 U.S. 805 (1971)
Prince v. Massachusetts, 321 U.S. 158 (1944)

R. v. R., 431 S.W. 2d (Mo. 1968)
Randolph v. Randolph, 146 Fla. 491, 1 So.2d 480 (1941)

Raymond v. Cotner, 175 Neb. 158, 120 N.W. 2d 892 (1963)
Reinhard v. Reinhard, 96 Wis. 555, 71 N.W. 803 (1897)
Rex v. Greenhill, 4 A. & E. 624 (1836)
Risting v. Sparboe, 179 Iowa 1133, 162 N.W. 592 (1917)
Roberts v. State, 82 Neb. 651, 118 N.W. 674 (1908)
Roe v. Bolton, 93 S.Ct. 739 (1973)
Roe v. Doe, 36 App.Div. 162, 318 N.Y.S. 2d 973 (1971)
Roe v. Wade, 93 S.Ct. 705 (1973)
Rouse v. State, 184 So. 2d 839 (Ala. App. 1966)

Scarpetta v. DiMartino, 254 So. 2d 813, aff'd 262 So. 2d 442 (1972),
     cert den. 404 U.S. 805 (1971).
Sheldon v. Springett, 11 C.B. 452 (1851)
Shelley v. Westbrooke, 37 Eng. Rep. 850 (Ch. 1817)
Smith v. Smith, 17 Ohio App.2d 4, 218 N.E. 2d 473 (1964)
Smith v. Smith, 15 Utah 2d 36, 386 P. 2d 900 (1963)
Stanley v. Illinois, 405 U.S. 645 (1972)
State *ex rel.* Fox v. Webster, 151 So.2d 14 (Fla.App. 1963)
State v. Garber, 197 Kan. 567, 419 P.2d 896 (1966)
State v. Marcri, 498 P.2d 355 (Utah 1972)
State v. Straight, 347 P.482 (Mont. 1959)
Steier v. N.Y. State Bd. of Ed., 271 F.2d 13 (C.A.2 1959)
Stehr v. State, 92 Neb. 755, 139 N.W. 676 (1913)
Sullivan v. Montgomery, 155 Misc. 448, 279 N.Y.S. 2d 575 (1935)

Tigner v. Texas, 310 U.S. 141 (1940)
Tinker v. Des Moines School Dist., 393 U.S. 503 (1969)

United States v. F.A. Darby Lumber Co., 312 U.S. 100 (1941)

Vlasak v. Vlasak, 204 Minn. 331, 283 N.W. 489 (1939)

Wack v. Wack, 74 N.Y.S. 2d 573 (1st Dept. 1944)
Wendland v. Wendland, 29 Wis. 2d 145, 138 N.W.2d 185 (1965)
Wolf v. Wolf, 194 App.Div. 33, 185 N.Y.S. 37 (1920)

Zinni v. Zinni, 238 A.2d 373 (R.I. 1968)

BIBLIOGRAPHY

Ackerman, Nathan: *The Psychodynamics of Family Life.* New York, Basic Books, 1958.

Alexander, Paul W.: Constitutional Rights in Juvenile Court. In Rosenhiem, Margaret F. (Ed.) : *Justice for the Child.* New York, Free Press, 1962.

Allen, Francis A.: *The Borderland of Justice.* Chicago, Univ. of Chicago Press, 1964.

Alternatives to parental right in custody disputes involving third persons. *Yale L J, 73:*151, 1963.

Baldwin, Alfred L.: *Theories of Child Development.* New York, John Wylie & Sons, 1968.

Benedek, Theresa: The psychosomatic implications of primary unit: Mother-child. *Am J of Orthopsych, 19:*642, 1949.

Blackstone, Erlich's ed. San Carlos, Nourse, 1959.

Blackstone's Commentaries, Gavit ed. Washington D.C., Washington Law Books, 1941.

Bodenheimer, Brigitte: Uniform child custody jurisdiction act. *Vand L Rev, 22:*1207, 1969.

Bowlby, Jahn: *Attachment and Loss.* New York, Basic Books, 1969.

Brockelbank, William and Infausto, Felix: *Interstate Enforcement of Family Support,* 2d ed. Indianapolis, Bobbs-Merrill, 1971.

Bryce, James: Marriage and Divorce Under Roman and English Law, *II Studies in History and Jurisprudence.* Freeport, Bks for Libs., 1961. Reprinted in *III Select Essays in Anglo-American History,* 1909.

Chess, Stella: *An Introduction to Child Psychiatry.* New York, Grune & Stratton, 1969.

Civil death—Medieval fiction in a modern world. *Harv L Rev, 50:*968, 1937.

Clark, Homer H., Jr.: *Law of Domestic Relations.* St. Paul, West, 1968.

Committee on Health Services Inside and Outside the Family Court in New York City, "Juvenile Justice Confounded: Pretensions and Realities in Treatment Services," 1972 Report.

Condit, H.V. and Liebenow, R.C.: Management of estates of minors and incompetents. *U Ill L F, 268,* 1951

Connolly, C.S.: Divorce Proctors. *B U L Rev, 34:*1, 1954.

Cox, Poston: The divorce proctor. *Tenn L Rev, 33:*439, 1966.

Custody Contests Between Parent and Grandparent, Annot. 25 *A L R* 3d 1 (1969).

Custody and control of children. *Fordham L Rev, 5:*460, 1936.

Davie, Ronald, Butler, Neville and Goldstein, Harvey: *From Birth to Seven.* London, Longman, 1972.

Despert, J. Louise: *Children of Divorce.* Garden City, Doubleday, 1962.

Divided custody of children after their parents divorce, *J Fam L, 8:*58, 1968.

Divorce reform act. *Harv Legis, 5:*563, 1968.

Dorsen, Norman and Rezneck, Daniel A.: In re Gault and the Future of Juvenile Law. *Fam L Q, 1:*1, 1967.

Drinan, Robert F.: The rights of children in modern American family law. *J Fam L, 2:*101, 1962.

Elder, Glen H.: Parental Power Legitimation and Its Effect on the Adolescent. Reprinted in Goldstein and Katz: *The Law and the Family.* New York, Free Press, 1965. p. 980.

English, O.S. and Finch, S.M.: *Emotional Problems of Growing Up.* Chicago, Science Research Associates, 1951.

English, O.S. and Foster, Constance: *Fathers are Parents Too.* New York, Putnam, 1951.

Erickson, Erik H.: *Childhood and Society,* 2d ed. New York, W.W. Norton, 1963.

Finch, Stuart M.: *Fundamentals of Child Psychiatry.* New York, W.W. Norton, 1960.

Forer, Lois: *No One Will Lissen.* New York, Grosset & Dunlap, 1971.

Foster, H.H.: Adoption and child custody: Best interests of the child?, *Buffalo L Rev, 22:*1, 1972.

Foster, H.H.: Annual survey of American family law. *N Y U L Rev, 36:*629, 1961.

Foster, H.H.: Dependent Children and the Law. *U Pitt L Rev, 18:*579, 1957.

Foster, H.H.: Marriage: A "Basic Civil Right of Man." *Fordham L Rev, 37:* 51, 1968.

Foster, H.H.: Notice and Fair Procedure: Revolution or Simple Revision?, ICLE, *Gault: What Now for the Juvenile Court?,* Virginia Davis Nordin, ed., 1968.

Foster, H.H.: Revocation of Consent to Adoption. *NYLJ,* Aug. 6, 1971.

Foster, H.H.: Social work, the law, and social action. *Social Casework,* July 1964.

Foster, H.H. and Freed, D.J.: A bill of rights for minors. *NYLJ,* July 28, Aug. 23, Sept. 29, 1972.

Foster, H.H. and Freed, D.J.: Child custody, *N Y U L Rev, 39:*423, 615, 1964.

Foster, H.H. and Freed, D.J.: *Law and the Family—New York,* rev. ed. Rochester, Lawyers-Co-operative, 1972.

Foster, H.H. and Freed, D.J.: Marital property reform: Partnership of co-equals? *NYLJ,* March 5, 23, April 27, 1973.

Foster, H.H. and Freed, D.J.: The Battered Child. *Trial, 3:*33, 1967.

Fraser, George B.: Guardianship of the person. *Iowa L Rev, 45:*239, 1960.

Fratcher, William F.: Powers and duties of guardians of property. *Iowa L Rev, 45*:264, 1960.

Freeman, Lucy and Hulse, Dr. Wilfred C.: *Children Who Kill.* New York, Berkeley Pub. Co., 1968.

Gardner, L.I.: Separation of the parents and the emotional life. *Mental Hygiene, 40*:53, 1956.

Gesell, Arnold: *The First Five Years of Life.* New York, Harper-Row, 1940; *The Child from Five to Ten.* New York, Harper-Row, 1946; and *Youth, the Years from Ten to Sixteen.* New York, Harper-Row, 1956.

Glueck, Sheldon and Gleuck, Eleanor: *The Problem of Delinquency.* Boston, Houghton-Mifflin, 1959.

Goldstein, Joseph and Katz, Jay: *The Family and the Law.* New York, Free Press, 1965.

Group for the Advancement of Psychiatry, series on Child Psychiatry.

Guttmacher, Manfred: *The Mind of the Murderer.* Freeport, Bks. for Libs., 1960.

Hansen, Robert: The role and rights of children in divorce actions. *J Fam L, 6*:1, 1966.

Hartz, Louis: *Economic Policy and Democratic Thought.* Cambridge, Harvard Univ. Press, 1948.

Herzog, E. and Vincent, C.: Who are the unmarried mothers? *Children, 9*: 157, 1962.

Holmes, O.W.: The Path of the Law. *Harv L Rev, 10*:457, 1897.

Inker, Monroe L.: Expanding the Rights of Children in Custody Cases. *J Fam L, 11*:129, 1971.

Jacobsen, Paul: *American Marriage and Divorce.* New York, Rinehart, 1959.

James, T.E.: The age of majority. *Am J Leg Hist, 4*:22, 1960.

Jones, Eve: *Raising Your Child in a Fatherless Home.* New York, Free Press, 1963.

Judicial Power to order medical treatment for minors. *Syracuse L Rev, 14*: 84, 1962.

Kanowitz, Leo: *Women and the Law.* Albuquerque, Univ. of New Mexico Press, 1969.

Katz, Jay and Goldstein, Joseph: *The Family and the Law.* New York, Free Press, 1965.

Katz, Sanford N.: *Parents Who Fail.* Boston, Beacon Press, 1971.

Kent, Chancellor James: *Commentaries on American Law,* Browne's ed. St. Paul, West, 1894.

Krause, Harry D.: Equal protection for the illegitimate. *Mich L Rev, 65*:477, 1967; Legitimate and illegitimate offspring of Levy v. Louisiana. *U Chic L Rev, 36*:338, 1969.

Krause, Harry D. : *Illegitimacy: Law and Social Policy.* Indianapolis, Bobbs-Merril, 1971.

Levy, John and Monroe, Ruth: *The Happy Family.* New York, Knopf, 1938.

Lord Acton, Letter to Bishop Mandell Creighton (1887) .

Mack, Julian W.: The juvenile court, *Harv L Rev, 23:*104, 1909.

Madden, J. Warren: *Persons and Domestic Relations.* St. Paul, West, 1931.

Mahler, Margaret S.: Discipline and Punishment (Reprinted in Goldstein and Katz, *The Family and the Law,* 977-980). New York, Free Press, 1965.

Metz, Charles V.: *Divorce and Custody for Men.* New York, Doubleday, 1968.

Midonick, Millard L.: *Children, Parents and the Courts.* New York, P.L.I., 1972.

McCoid, Allan H.: Battered child. *Minn L Rev, 50:*1, 1965.

McCurdy, William: Torts between parent and child. *Vill L Rev, 5:*521, 1960.

Nelson, Lawrence J.: Right of a teacher to administer corporal punishment to a student. *Washburn L J, 5:*75, 1965.

Neurotic Interaction in Marriage, the *Psychoanalytic Study of the Family,* Flugel, ed. New York, Hillary, 1954.

New York Education Law

New York Family Court Act

Note, Divided Custody of Children After Their Parents Divorce, *J Fam L., 8:*58, 1968.

N.Y.C.L.U.: *Student Rights Handbook for N.Y.C.,* 1972.

Oster, Alan M.: Custody proceeding: A study of vague and indefinite standards. *J Fam L, 5:*21, 1965.

Painter, Hal: *Mark I Love You.* New York, Simon & Schuster, 1967.

Patton, R.G. and Gardner, L.I.: *Growth Failure in Maternal Deprivation.* Springfield, Thomas, 1963.

Paulsen, Monrad: Kent v. United, 1966 *Sup Ct. Rev.* 167.

Paulsen, Monrad: The legal framework for child protection. *Col L Rev, 66:* 679, 1966.

Paulsen, Monard, Parker, Graham and Adelman, Lynn: Child abuse reporting laws—Some legislative history. *Geo. Wash L Rev, 34:*482, 1966.

Plant, J.S.: The psychiatrist views children of divorced parents. *Law Contemp Prob, 10:*807, 1944.

Ploscowe, Morris, Foster, H.H. and Freed, D.J.: *Family Law,* rev. ed. Boston, Little, Brown, 1972.

Pollock, Sir Frederick and Maitland, Frederic W.: *History of English Law,* 2d ed. Washington, D.C., Lawyer's Literary Club, 1959.

Prosser, William L.: *Law of Torts,* 3d ed. St. Paul, West, 1964.

Prosser, William L.: *Law of Torts,* 4th ed. St. Paul, West, 1971.

Report of the President's Commission on Law Enforcement and Administration of Justice, Task Force on Juvenile Justice. "Juvenile Justice and Youth Crime" (1967).

Robitscher, Jonas: Courts, state hospitals, and the right to treatment. *Am J of Psych, 129:*3, 1972.

Robitscher, Jonas: Statutes, Law Enforcement, and the Judicial Process. In Resnick, H.L.P. and Wolfgang, Marvin: *Sexual Behavior: Social, Clinical, and Legal Aspects.* Boston, Little, Brown, 1972.

Roche, Philip Q.: *The Criminal Mind.* New York, Grove Press, 1959.

Rubin, Sol: Children as victims of institutionalization. *Child Welfare, 60:*6, 1972.

Saint Augustine, Code of Canon Law, 3d ed., 1923.

Seavey, Warren A.: Dismissal of students: "Due Process." *Harv L Rev, 70:* 1406, 1957.

Sidman, L.R.: The Massachusetts Stubborn Child Law. *Fam L Q, 6:*33, 1972.

Simon, A.W.: *Stepchild in the Family.* New York, Simon & Schuster, 1964.

Skard, A.G.: Maternal deprivation: The research and its implication. *J Marr Fam, 27:*333, 1965.

Speca, John and Wehrman, R.L.: Protecting the rights of children in divorce cases in Missouri. *U M K C L Rev, 38:*1, 1969.

Spitz, Rene: Hospitalization, an Inquiry into the Genesis of Psychiatric Conditions in Early Childhood. In *The Psychoanalytic Study of the Child,* Vol. I. New York, Int. University Press, 1945.

Stolz, L.M.: *Father Relations of War Born Children.* Stanford, Stanford Univ. Press, 1954.

Tenney, Charles W., Jr.: Sex, sanity, and stupidity in Massachusetts. *B U L Rev, 42:*1, 1962.

Termination of parental rights to free a child for adoption. *N Y U L Rev, 32:*579, 1957.

The Absence of the Father. *Am J of Orthopsych, 29:*644, 1959.

Uniform Interstate Compact on Juveniles.

Uniform Marriage and Divorce Act, 1971.

United Nation Declaration of Rights of Children.

Vincent, Clark: *Unmarried Mothers.* New York, Free Press, 1961.

Watson, Andrew: *Psychiatry for Lawyers.* New York, Int. University Press, 1968.

White House Conference on Child Health and Protection, 1930.

Williston on Contracts, Vol. II, Chap. 9, 3d ed. Mt. Kisco, Baker-Voorhis, 1959.

Wiss, Harriett: Position Paper on Medical Care of Minors, N.Y.U. Conference on Children and the Law, 1971.

Wylie, H.L. and Delgado, R.A.: A pattern of mother-son relationships involving the absence of the father. *Am J of Orthopsych, 29:*644, 1959.

Wright, Charles: The constitution on the campus. *Vand L Rev, 22:*1027, 1969.

Young, Leontine: *Out of Wedlock.* New York, McGraw, 1954.

INDEX